MEANINGFUL PERFORMANCE REVIEWS

1 / YOUR ADVISOR

MEANINGFUL PERFORMANCE REVIEWS

SEÁN McLOUGHNEY

Published in 2014 by
Chartered Accountants Ireland
Chartered Accountants House
47–49 Pearse Street
Dublin 2
www.charteredaccountants.ie

ISBN 978-1-908199-78-2

Typeset by PH Media
Printed by GRAFO, S.A.

For Carol, Alex and Rachel and my parents, Seán and Anne.

ONTENTS

ACKNOWLEDGEMENTS

Sitting in front of your laptop staring at a blank page is never fun for any author, but perhaps the hardest part of the job for me is trying to convey in a few sentences the debt of gratitude I owe to so many people. Although writing a book is a solidary exercise for 90% of the time, it is in the final straight that the team of experts come aboard and weave their magic. I would like to take this opportunity to thank the many people that have worked tirelessly on this project. As always I am eternally grateful to Michael Diviney (Director of Publishing) for his calmness, faith in my ideas, and challenging me to make it better. Dan Bolger took on the massive task of editing and proofreading the manuscript, a skill that is essential to this project and I am so fortunate that he is a master of his trade. Thanks are also due to Iain Whitelegge of PH Media, who designed the book.

This project would never have seen the light of day without the unwavering support of my wife Carol, who kept me going with her words of encouragement and practical advice. Extra special thanks must go to the best two girls in the world, our daughters Alex and Rachel. My parents Sean and Anne were, as always, there to support this venture in so many different ways, as were Geraldine and Kevin.

I would also like to thank the thousands of people who have attended my workshops over the years. They are the people who have tired, tested and challenged my ideas, tips and templates that are used throughout this book. Their continuous endorsement of my training workshops and in particular my ideas keep me inspired and excited about this job of mine. I would also like to thank all the people who have helped me with my research for this project. In particular I would like to thank the following people for going the extra yard and sharing their expertise with me: Aidan Meagher, Brendan Deeney, Ken Tyrrell, Rory O'Hare, Rory Meehan, Gordon Lynn, Ronan Mac Giolla Phadraig, Sara Dowling, Kevin Hannigan, Gerry Cleary, Martin Downes, Steve Foley, Andy O'Callaghan and Dave Fitzgerald. My thanks also to all my clients that I have worked with and for their continuing support over the years. I hope you enjoy the book and, most of all, I hope it helps you become a great leader.

CHAPTER ONE

THE NEED FOR CHANGE

1

IT HAPPENS "Alex, fill out that appraisal form for me and have it on my desk before you go home. Your review meeting is at 10am tomorrow. We won't need much time – 20 or 30 minutes should do it. HR are hassling me to have all the forms back to them by Friday. Tell the others to complete their appraisal forms as well; I'll e-mail them their times later today. The sooner we get this out of the way, the better. Such a waste of time – aren't you all great anyway?"

The dreaded annual performance review

If the above scenario sounds familiar, then you, like many others, face some serious challenges. Although performance management has been around in some form for decades, managers still struggle with its complexities. A survey carried out by the Chartered Institute of Personnel and Development (CIPD) found that only 20% of respondents agree that "performance management has a positive impact on individual performance".

'Wasteful' and 'frustrating' are the words most likely to be used to describe what should be the most important meeting of the year for managers and their teams, as review meetings have become annual form-filling exercises that have little or no impact on people's performance levels. The question is, then: why are people still participating in review meetings that simply don't work?

In most cases, the meetings are held because they are an annual requirement imposed by senior management. Perhaps at first there was support for managers and staff by way of some basic training on how to run the review meeting effectively and all parties put in the effort to ensure its success. After the initial enthusiasm, however, the slow death march began, and the whole process became one long box-ticking exercise, an annual ritual that people see no merit in.

In the last 10 years or more, the art of managing people has evolved in many ways. Traditionally, people were promoted based on their technical ability, depth of experience and knowledge. In the early 19th century, Henri Fayol, a French mining engineer and one of the first writers to explore the role of managers, defined the functions of management in terms of five elements. He believed that the purpose of management "is to forecast and plan, to organise, to command, to coordinate and to control". While the ability to plan, organise and control the workflow will always be important, these skills, on their own, are no longer sufficient.

TO FORECAST AND PLAN

TO ORGANISE

TO COMMAND

TO COORDINATE

TO CONTROL

Today, managing people successfully also requires great leadership skills. Managers need to engage, inspire and create a culture of high performance in their team. Talented people expect their managers to communicate regularly with them and discuss how their work impacts the business. Involving them in some day-to-day decisions will increase ownership of these tasks. This in turn will have a positive effect on productivity levels.

A competitive business environment brings new challenges and concerns, which can be overcome with a better understanding of business needs and by working collaboratively with your team to resolve issues and focus on key priorities. Achieving business targets means managing people in smarter ways than ever before.

From a performance perspective, the role of the manager, whatever their rank, is to integrate performance review meetings into the day-to-day activities of the team. Managers need to take responsibility for turning the dreaded annual review into a tool for helping their team achieve expected results on a continuous basis.

A good place to start this transformation is to answer some important basic questions about review meetings:

What is the purpose of our review meetings?

What benefits should we get from our review meetings?

What are the 'success indicators' for our review meetings?

FIGURE 1.1 — REVIEW MEETING SUCCESS INDICATORS

ANSWER THE FOLLOWING QUESTION:

A YEAR FROM NOW, WHAT WILL BE MY APPROACH TO THE TEAM'S REVIEW MEETINGS?

Define what success looks like for their review meetings. Start with some 'what if' questions that could lead to a new approach:

- What if my team left their review meeting fully engaged and inspired to achieve great things?
- What if my team fully understood their role and what is expected of them?
- What if my team sets their own goals that were aligned to the business plan and exceed my expectations?
- What if my team took responsibility for their learning and development?
- What if my team had quarterly review meetings?

Distil the 'success indicators' into a couple of short sentences. For example, describe how you and your team would prepare for them, the best way to run a meeting and what outcomes a successful meeting would deliver.

Rethink your approach to review meetings

"Our mission statement about treating people with respect and dignity is not just words but a creed we live by every day. You can't expect your employees to exceed the expectations of your customers if you don't exceed the employees' expectations of management."

HOWARD SCHULTZ, CEO OF STARBUCKS

When it comes to exceeding "employees' expectations of management", one critical area that managers can improve upon is the way performance review meetings are conducted. They provide managers with a great platform to communicate expectation levels and clarify priorities. Failing to invest the necessary time to prepare, execute and follow through on these meetings will undermine their creditability. If you don't take them seriously, then don't expect your team to.

There is also a practical business reason to rethink your approach to review meetings. The quality of its staff is a key component to the long-term success of a business. As staffing levels become tighter, managers are expected to maximise performance levels of all their people. If upwards of 90% of your organisation's performance depends on how you manage your staff, then it's time to reassess your approach to traditional performance review meetings. Engaged and high-performing people take responsibility for their performance and understand what is expected of them. During their review meeting there is a real focus on how they will achieve their business and personal goals. According to a 2011 report by Mercer, "Employee engagement is seen as having the most significant impact on organisation financial performance, customer service and quality."

Performance review meetings are about more than just discussing people's targets and key objectives (see Figure 1.2). They should underpin a culture of high performance and results. They also play an important role in retaining your best people as they provide an ideal opportunity for a manager to discuss their future plans for each individual. It's a platform to discuss career progression.

FIGURE 1.2 — REVIEW MEETING: BENEFITS SNAPSHOT

REVIEW MEETINGS SHOULD ENSURE THAT EMPLOYEES:

- Understand their goals and how they are aligned to the overall business strategy.
- Are given feedback on their performance and shown where they add real value to the organisation.
- Have the necessary skills and knowledge to exceed their goals and deliver high performance.
- Are part of the process of defining their goals.
- Can demonstrate why they are the best at what they do and what they will achieve this year.
- Are thinking like entrepreneurs in the workplace and have a positive impact on the business strategy.
- Understand what is expected of them, both in terms of results and how those results should be achieved.
- Are part of your talent management system and managing their own career development.
- Feel that their individual contribution is recognised and appreciated
- Have an opportunity to demonstrate what additional value they bring to the team.
- Feel excited, energised and enthused about their role in the team.

Employees understand their goals and how these are aligned to the overall business strategy

All of your team's effort and energy must be focused on achieving the overall business goals. Failure to clearly communicate what objectives are important will result in some of your team being busy doing the wrong things. A core objective of the review meeting is to ensure that everyone on your team understands the difference between being busy and being productive.

Carefully consider how and when to communicate your organisation's business goals. It is the role of the manager to translate the business strategy at its highest level into what it means for the team. This ensures that all discussions around goals have some context.

Employees are given feedback on their performance and shown where they add real value

Timely feedback underpins a high-performance culture. It is vital if an individual wants to improve his or her performance. However, giving and receiving feedback can be a minefield. A well-planned and structured approach is needed to avoid common pitfalls, such as the feedback being too vague or overly personal. What might start out as a conversation to boost morale and confidence could very quickly degenerate into a confrontation, resulting in a demotivated person leaving the meeting.

Feedback is often linked to negativity and criticism. Most people are given feedback on what went wrong and rarely given feedback on what they are doing right. Over time, this approach will affect morale and ultimately performance.

Just because you know the value that someone brings to the team and your organisation doesn't mean that they do. People need to know that their efforts make a real difference. Obviously, people need to be aware if something they did isn't up to the required standard or if they are applying their efforts in the wrong areas – but make sure to balance giving corrective feedback by heaping praise when it is deserved. Be careful that you don't underestimate the importance of giving praise, including to your high performers.

The necessity of showing appreciation also applies to tasks that are often perceived as being 'low value'. Truly engaged people are given regular feedback on how even their routine work is adding value. There is a significant difference between "I input figures into a spreadsheet all day" and "I provide timely and accurate information to senior management so that they can make effective, business critical decisions."

Employees have the necessary skills and knowledge to exceed their goals and deliver high performance

High-performing people combine the right attitude with the necessary skills and knowledge to do the job. Investing in a systematic and thoughtful learning and development plan will positively affect the performance levels of your team. In his book, *The Starbucks Experience*, Joseph Michelli points out that "the Starbucks business model calls for spending more on training than on advertising. As a result it enjoys an excellent rate of employee retention and thereby continues the connection between its partners (staff) and customers." Investing in the right people delivers long-term benefits and helps your organisation to become an employer of choice for talented workers.

Employees are part of the process of defining their key business goals

Being involved in defining the team's business goals will increase personal accountability by fostering a sense of ownership.

"Research indicates that workers have three prime needs: interesting work, recognition for doing a good job, and being let in on things that are going on in the company."

ZIG ZIGLAR

One of the important "things that are going on in the company" is the business plan. Discuss it with your team prior to your next review meetings. This is an opportunity to outline what your priorities are and where focus should be. Involve your team in translating the business plan into tasks for the team.

Employees can demonstrate why they are the best at what they do and what they will achieve this year

The review meeting is an ideal opportunity for individuals to highlight their successes during the review period and how these contributed to the business results of your organisation. It also allows a manager to assess what activities people believe are important and how they are prioritising them.

When people understand how their efforts contribute to the success of the business, they are more likely to bring passion and drive to their performance. A review meeting provides managers with the opportunity to combine this understanding with recognition that their efforts are important.

Another key component of the meeting is the discussion around the area that each team member will focus on for the next period. The team leader will learn what everyone intends to do and how they will optimise their time and resources.

Employees are thinking like entrepreneurs in the workplace and have a positive impact on the business strategy

One of the 'Success Indicators' for a review meeting is encouraging your team to think like entrepreneurs in the workplace. By doing so, they will attend their meeting fully prepared and ready to take on additional responsibilities. Entrepreneurs in the workplace are always endeavouring to improve work practices, build better customer relations and find ways to have a positive impact on the business strategy. Their enthusiasm needs to be encouraged while at the same time controlled; a maverick entrepreneur in your team can sometimes have a negative effect as they may introduce changes without your approval or without considering the impact on others.

Employees understand what is expected of them, in terms of results and how they should be achieved

Whether your team is large or small, regular reviews will help to create a culture of communicating your expectations for performance within your team. While it is common for staff to understand their key objectives, there can be confusion over how they should be achieved. It takes time and effort to articulate your expectations in a way that your team will fully understand both what they should do and how they should do it. In addition to helping your team understand your expectations, you also need to provide adequate guidance so that performance can be measured fairly.

Employees are involved in managing their career development

During the review meeting, encourage each member of your team to think about their career plans and discuss how you and the organisation can support them. It is a great opportunity for a manager to identify the high flyers and ensure that they are proactive in developing themselves. Increasingly, there is more emphasis placed on retaining talented people because resources are tight and talented people add significantly more to the bottom line.

Employees feel that their individual contribution is recognised and appreciated

While the main focus throughout the year is on achieving results, there is a need to sit down with people and outline how their individual contribution has impacted the business. Taking some time out of busy schedules and showing genuine appreciation for their efforts builds engagement and commitment.

Employees have an opportunity to demonstrate what additional value they bring to the team

An opportunity that is often missed in a meeting is a discussion around the additional value that a person brings to the team. For example, someone may help a new person to integrate quickly into the team, build the morale or simply fix the photocopier when it breaks down. Celebrate their individualism.

Employees feel excited, energised and enthused about their role in the team
Without doubt the most important benefit is that everyone should leave the meeting excited, energised and enthused about their work. As hotelier and author Orison Swett Marden puts it: "Just make up your mind at the very outset that your work is going to stand for quality; that you are going to stamp a superior quality upon everything that goes out of your hands; that whatever you do shall bear the hallmark of excellence."

Challenges to overcome

"I have learned that success is to be measured not so much by the position that one has reached in life as by the obstacles which he has overcome while trying to succeed."

AMERICAN EDUCATOR BOOKER T. WASHINGTON

Successfully dealing with the numerous challenges that can be experienced with review meetings will help you achieve your business goals. It is acknowledged that there are polarised views about review meetings – they can be viewed as either an opportunity to improve performance levels or an annual nuisance. Whatever your view, it is most likely that review meetings are here to stay.

Despite their obvious importance and even if you are an advocate, there are a number of challenges that managers need to address, including those listed in Figure 1.3:

FIGURE 1.3 — CHALLENGES TO REVIEW MEETINGS

NEGATIVE EMPLOYEE MINDSET

FORM-FILLING EXERCISE

NOT ENOUGH TIME

DISCONNECT FROM GOALS

APATHY FROM SENIOR MANAGERS

VAGUE KEY BUSINESS PRIORITIES

LACK OF CLEAR PERFORMANCE-RATING CRITERIA

THE 'HALO EFFECT'

IT'S ALL ABOUT THE RECENT PERFORMANCE

ITS ONLY PURPOSE IS TO DETERMINE BONUSES

Negative employee mindset

Perhaps the biggest challenge to overcome is a negative employee mindset. It is common in someone who has lost all interest in their job, and can drain the energy and enthusiasm from everyone else. Their favourite phrases are 'that's not my job' or 'that's above my salary level'. They will attend a review meeting with limited preparation, totally disinterested in the meeting. In their view they are completely overloaded with tasks already and now you are going to lumber them with additional work. As far as they are concerned, the whole process is a waste of time and unfair.

Form-filling exercise

Many managers still consider the review meeting to be a form-filling exercise that only benefits the people in human resources, a once a year bureaucratic process that has little or no impact on performance or how they manage their team. The agenda for the meeting is dictated by the forms and questions are asked merely to fill in each section. In many cases the forms are even completed prior to the meeting and very little discussion takes place.

This approach puts the emphasis on the forms, which is a major distraction from the real purpose of the meeting. In some cases the manager isn't entirely to blame, as the forms can be up to twenty pages long. It is further compounded by the overuse of generic sections such as 'attention to detail', 'showing initiative' or 'communication'.

Not enough time

'I'm busy preparing end-of-year accounts' is a common excuse for not putting in the time to do the meetings properly. Sufficient time must be given to the review meetings to support the idea that they are part of the day-to-day activities of the team, rather than an interruption to busy schedules. It is also important to avoid cancelling meetings, as this will reinforce the belief that they aren't important and will only happen if there is enough time.

Disconnect from goals

An important challenge to overcome is the disconnect between the company's overall objectives and the goals set for individuals. It is not uncommon for organisations to perform poorly while most of their employees, according to the appraisals, meet and even exceed expectations. The question that is rarely asked is: "How can so many people be doing an excellent job if the company is performing poorly?" Such lack of alignment can have serious consequences.

Another major disconnect from the individual goals is that they are set at the start of the year, sometimes before the company goals are even agreed. Within a few months many of these goals are obsolete or deferred because the company goals have changed. Rarely are they updated, so people naturally lose interest because they believe that their efforts won't be recognised at the end-of-year review.

In other situations, people fail to see the benefit or need for some of their goals. They are given random objectives simply so that something can be entered on their review form.

Apathy from senior managers

If senior managers believe that review meetings are a waste of time, then it will be very hard to convince employees to take them seriously. Even where senior managers see the benefits of conducting regular review meetings, any lack of real commitment and enthusiasm can undermine the whole process.

Vague key business priorities

Your team won't be able to deliver a top performance if your key business targets and objectives are vague. If review meetings are conducted without the business plan ever being discussed with the team, how will they know what the year's key business objectives are?

IT HAPPENS

Professor Willie Pietersen of Columbia Business School in New York City, carried out research in an organisation where he was asked to improve how they implemented their business strategy. He discovered that the employees simply didn't know what was expected of them and everyone was similarly vague when asked about the key priorities for their organisation. "The results were startling. Very few employees could give a simple explanation of the company's strategy. More to the point, when I asked if they could offer a compelling reason why customers should choose to do business with their company, most gave vague, rambling answers; a few even looked surprised by the question. Perhaps most important, no one was clear what the key priorities were for the organisation or where their department fitted into that picture. Needless to say, there was not much excitement around the place."

Lack of clear performance-rating criteria

Confusion around rating criteria can lead to problems such as inconsistencies in the ratings obtained by co-workers and disillusionment where someone expected a higher score for their hard work. In many organisations the rating matrix is either too subjective or overly focused on results. Relying on human judgement alone can lead to feelings of bias.

Another challenge to overcome is the scoring mechanism itself – using the 1 to 5 scoring system causes a lot of problems as most people will achieve a score of 3. The problem here is that most staff perceive this score as average and they feel their performance was better than average. Management, on the other hand, views a score of 3 as meaning the person has achieved all of their goals. This problem is compounded by putting a limit on the number of people who can exceed expectations.

IT HAPPENS

Here is an example of the scoring system explained in a staff handbook of a company employing over 500 people.

"We have a scoring system of 1 to 5, with 5 being outstanding and 1 being unacceptable. It is envisaged that the distribution for bonus and pay progression will be as follows:

- Max 5% of people should receive a 5
- Max 10% of people should receive a 4
- At least 5% of people should be allocated to the bottom two and will be on performance improvement plans or disciplinary procedures
- The balance of employees would be in the 3 category."

If you cap the number of people who can exceed expectation (in the above case 75 people), you are limiting the level of performance that can be achieved. Why would your entire team aim to exceed expectations if they knew from the start that only 5% of them could achieve a score of 5? What happens if 250 people clearly exceeded expectations? What impact will it have on next year's performance? How many of the 250 people will stay?

The 'halo effect'

The human factor can also play a role in distorting the evaluation of someone's performance. When a team is small and everyone gets on well with each other, the challenge is to separate personalities from performance. The key question here is, "Do I like this person because he or she is a good worker or do I merely think this person is a good worker because I like him or her?" Conversely, if someone on the team is disliked or doesn't participate in the team's social activities, will their performance be viewed poorly based on their personality rather than their results?

It's all about the recent performance

Annual reviews also run the risk of focusing too much on recent performance. For example, say in the last quarter one of your team delivers an outstanding performance and achieves some great results. The fact that their performance during the first three quarters was poor to average is forgotten and this person is given a high rating. On the other hand, this person could have had a poor final two months to the year and as a result the other 10 months of excellent work are overlooked.

Its only purpose is to determine bonuses

A common perception of review meetings is that their sole purpose is to determine wage increases and bonuses. The rest of the conversation around performance and goals is therefore overlooked, as the person is only interested in discussing their bonus. This linkage can cause problems when times are tough and there are no wages increases as people will view the meetings as pointless.

IT HAPPENS I was asked to run some training workshops on improving performance review meetings for a medium-sized company. The session with the management team went well; lots of enthusiasm and willingness to implement new frameworks. However, there was a different attitude from the staff. What I discovered was that the review meetings hadn't taken place in over three years because there were no bonuses or pay increases. Naturally, during the workshop I was consistently asked why should they bother doing review meetings when there was no likelihood of bonuses being paid. They were looking for an answer to the "What's in it for me?" question. It took a lot of persuading to convince them that review meeting are about more than simply determining bonuses.

Why do people participate in poor review meetings?

There are a variety of reasons why intelligent people waste so much time by participating in poor review meetings that don't work. For many it's a combination of factors, while for others it has happened gradually over time. As a result they are probably unaware of the negative impact that poor review meetings have on their team.

The most common reasons for participating in negative review meetings are as shown in Figure 1.4.

These excuses are not intended to be a complete list; you may have your own reasons for participating in poor review meetings. Whatever the reason, one thing is certain: you need to start to take responsibility for improving the effectiveness of your review meetings.

FIGURE 1.4 — THE MOST COMMON REASONS FOR PARTICIPATING IN NEGATIVE REVIEW MEETING

THE MOST COMMON REASONS FOR PARTICIPATING IN NEGATIVE REVIEW MEETINGS
The boss told them that they had to do the review meetings by a certain date.
It's required in order to be considered for future career advancement.
They could lose their job if they refuse.
Everyone else is doing them.
The team wants them.
HR are hassling them for the forms.
Revenge on the team, an opportunity. to slam someone.
"Don't rock the boat".
They don't have a better way to determine bonuses and pay increases.

There is a better way

The high-performing leaders of the next 20 years must embrace the role that performance review meetings will play in managing their teams. People want to know how their work impacts the business strategy and that they add value to their organisation; they require real leadership and an inspiring work environment.

Despite the bad press associated with performance review meetings, there is a better way to approach them that will ensure success. The many constraints that can overwhelm even the most enthusiastic manager must be dealt with in a systematic and focused way. Kimberly-Clark, the company behind well-known brands such as Huggies nappies, Andrex toilet paper and other familiar products, faced up the challenge of flat sales and stagnant performance by developing a high-performance culture. Gary Short, a senior talent management consultant, explains that "in the end we came up with four principles: clarity, so that people are setting objectives and know what to do; alignment, so that those objectives are aligned to the business; accountability, so that we're doing what we say we're doing; and differentiation, because we hadn't been differentiating or really addressing performance issues."

FIGURE 1.5 — THE KIMBERLY-CLARK WAY

KIMBERLY-CLARK WAY			
CLARITY	ALIGNMENT	ACCOUNTABILITY	DIFFERENTIATION

PEAK Leadership for successful review meetings

PEAK Leadership is a framework I developed over the years to underpin how you can manage the performance of your team. Utilising a range of methods, tools and techniques that can be harnessed to optimise the benefits of performance reviews, it is based on four separate but interdependent principles.

First, you must continuously challenge your team's current level of performance. Asking people to do more when resources are tight isn't challenging performance, it is more likely to cause stress and become counterproductive. You need to challenge people by giving them some actionable direction: "Do this and we'll get this task completed, do that and we'll get that task completed next." In this way you can also encourage individual responsibility by asking, "How would you approach this task? Is there a better way of doing it?"

Secondly, you must create an environment in which challenging performance is seen as healthy and is embraced by all. Inspirational leaders can push people to reach their full potential. They work hard at being supportive and provide the necessary help to achieve expected goals. When appropriate, they empower their team to make the right decisions. The team have bought into their vision and they are trusted by the team. They believe in their manager's ability to deliver the desired results for business. They also understand how the company's success can benefit them individually.

Thirdly, it is essential that everyone's goals are aligned to the overall business strategy. All of your team must be pulling in the same direction. Good management is about your ability to keep the team aligned and ready to execute. People need to see and understand the connection between their work and the impact it has on the overall success of the team and organisation.

FIGURE 1.6 — THE PEAK LEADERSHIP FRAMEWORK

FIGURE 1.7 — PEAK LEADERSHIP

P

PERFORMANCE IS CHALLENGED

The business world should borrow the mantra used by top sportspeople: "Today's record is tomorrow's standard." Successful team leaders are constantly challenging the performance levels set by themselves and their team. Encouraging people to examine if their performance levels are the best they can produce is healthy for a team. Business is simple: if you aren't raising the bar, then your competitors will – and they will start eating into your market share. Getting ahead is difficult enough, staying ahead separates the best from everyone else.

E

ENVIRONMENT IS CREATED

In order to successfully challenge performance levels, you must ensure that the environment is right for doing so. People should feel comfortable giving and receiving feedback, setting standards for behaviour and interaction within the team. Everyone should believe that the performance levels required are achievable and necessary for the success of the team. Otherwise you will be deemed too demanding, never happy and in some cases you might come across as a bully. A high-performing environment is created over time and requires planning and effort. It doesn't happen by chance.

A

ALIGN THE GOALS

A high-performing environment only works if the results achieved are aligned to the overall business plan. Working smarter rather than harder by creating goal synergy is a primary benefit of goal alignment. Align the goal, focus the effort and then execute.

KEEP STAFF ENGAGED

Research shows that top performers are highly engaged. They are passionate and excited about their work and set themselves high standards. As a team leader, inspire and enable your team to reach their full potential.

Finally, using PEAK Leadership can help you to keep your team engaged, committed and focused on the desired results. Keeping your team engaged means that they will be driven to exceed the goals that are aligned to the business strategy. Success builds momentum and will create the right environment in which leaders can challenge their team's performance levels to achieve even greater success. PEAK Leadership provides you with the framework to manage your team and can also be used to help run successful review meetings.

You can start the process of embedding PEAK Leadership into your day-to-day activities through some self-reflection. This requires you to develop the daily practice of thinking about how to challenge your team's performance and how to create the right environment to challenge them. For example, a quick conversation with your team to discuss their priorities for the day, what support they need, what is coming down the track and acknowledging their progress. When you are driving your team forward, you must also ask yourself: is the total effort aligned to the overall business strategy?

Every day, ask yourself how you will keep your team engaged – maintaining high performance requires constant improvement and reassessment. Each principle in PEAK Leadership builds on the others and promotes high standards of work.

Hope is not a sustainable strategy

Every day there are numerous challenges facing busy team leaders, and one of them is getting the maximum performance out of every member of their team. This requires persistence, leadership and a well-defined process. Rick Page explains the title of his bestselling book about sales, *Hope is not a Strategy*, as follows: "I believe that hope, along with faith and love, are essential to life. Hope is what you do when you have no control. But a strategy is made up of actions and tactics that convert visions to results for those that can make things happen." Hoping that your review meetings will change and be more effective is not a strategy. It's time to take responsibility and start to implement some actions and techniques that will deliver results.

AT A GLANCE — CHAPTER ONE

If upwards to 90% of your organisation's performance depends on how you manage your staff, then it's time to reassess your approach to the traditional performance review meetings.

Review meetings are important because they communicate key business objectives, establish and agree expected results, assess current performance level, identify staff learning and development training needs, and support career management while providing consistent feedback. Despite their obvious importance and even if you are already an advocate, there are a number of challenges that team leaders need to address, including:

- Negative employee mindset
- Form-filling exercise
- Not enough time
- Disconnect from goals
- Apathy from senior managers
- Vague key business priorities
- Lack of clear performance-rating criteria
- The 'halo effect'
- It's all about the recent performance
- Its only purpose is to determine bonuses

Despite the bad press associated with performance review meetings, there is a better way that will ensure success. Hoping that your review meetings will change and be more effective is not a strategy; you need to create a plan of action to ensure that everyone benefits from them. Use the PEAK Leadership framework to guide your performance reviews – it utilises a range of methods, tools and techniques to optimise the benefits of performance reviews.

CHAPTER TWO

CHANGE THE MINDSET, CHANGE THE RESULTS

IT HAPPENS

Although performance reviews are meant to be motivational and a fair assessment c someone's overall performance in the year, there can be a point in the meetin where it turns into an emotional conversation about each other's views of the performance This biased conversation is often about issues that were dealt with at the time but resurfac at the meeting in a misguided effort on the manager's part to bring some balance to th review. Revisiting areas of underperformance that are no longer an issue is fostering blame culture mentality. Review meetings that spend too much time discussing the pas particularly problem areas, are a waste of time and energy. Quite often people sto participating in them and just sit there, waiting for next year's goals to be announced. The degenerate into a one-way conversation that will have no impact on performance levels.

It's time to question the logic

Performance review meetings should be more about the future than the past. The focus at every meeting needs to be on how your staff will deliver a high performance. You can't change the past, but you can influence the future performance of your team. Management consultant and author Peter Drucker observed that successful businesses are guided by the principle that "results are obtained by exploiting opportunities, not by solving problems. All that one can hope to get by solving a problem is to restore normality. All one can hope, at best, is to eliminate a restriction on the capacity of the business to obtain results. The results themselves must come from the exploitation of opportunities."

Moving to regular meetings that are based on opportunities for achieving results will create an environment in which your team will prosper and grow. Although problems do need to be fixed, discussing them at length in a review meeting isn't productive. Address these issues when they occur, but don't waste too much time fixing things that may not produce outstanding results.

The review meeting should answer some fundamental business questions about results, for example: what are your team's success indicators for this year and how will they achieve them? How do these success indicato fit into the organisation's overall strategy? En courage your team to think strategically an consider how they add value to the team. In spire them to behave like entrepreneurs i the workplace and to take responsibility fc their results. From a pragmatic viewpoint, better performance from your team will tran late into a greater return for you.

For more than a decade I have delivere workshops to thousands of people to hel improve their performance levels. At thes sessions I always start with two simple que tions that are based on some sound busine principles. The first question I pose is, "Woul you run a business without a business plan The answer so far has always been the sam – of course not. Your plan outlines yo business goals and targets; it gives you sense of direction and purpose and identifie critical business challenges. It is a bluepri for success and a roadmap to help you mana your business effectively. A well-thought-o plan builds confidence in your ability to deliv your vision and charts the specific actio you will take to improve the performance your business. Committing your plan to pap will help you focus your energy and skills c achieving key results. A good business pl will also contain critical benchmarks that will help you monitor your progress. Over the years the reasons for writing a business plan haven't changed, and it's still seen as good business practice.

The second question I ask is, "Would you turn up at a meeting with your most important customer with little or no preparation, especially if the sole purpose of this meeting was to convince the customer to continue doing business with you despite intense competition from other suppliers?" Again, the answer to this question is a consistent no, because it would be unprofessional and you would most likely end up losing the contract. They also go on to say that they would spend as much time as possible planning this meeting, leaving nothing to chance. Most people would class this question as a 'no brainer'.

It is quite obvious from these workshops that you wouldn't run a business without a business plan and you certainly wouldn't visit your most important client without thorough preparation. Yet, remarkably, employees still approach their performance review meetings with little preparation or strategic planning. They fail to use these basic business principles and apply them to their own review meetings. Most employees are unable or unwilling to see the connection between writing a business plan for an organisation and writing one for their performance reviews. To compound this problem, their preparation time for their review meeting is, on average, no more than 30 minutes. What do they believe can be achieved in these 30 minutes?

IN THESE 30 MINUTES, PEOPLE BELIEVE THAT THEY CAN PLAN HOW THEY WILL:	
Outline why their performance over the last 12 months would warrant a bonus or wage increase.	
Anticipate any underperformance issues and be in a position to convince their manager that the issue won't reoccur.	
Set goals that are aligned to the overall business strategy.	
Discuss their personal development requirements.	
Discuss their career aspirations and how the company can support their ambitions.	
Demonstrate how they will add value to the team over the coming 12 months.	
Demonstrate that they are ready to take on additional responsibilities within the team.	
Review last year's report and make appropriate comments.	

Transitioning to the PEAK Leadership approach for review meetings

Review meetings don't need to be complex or cause anxiety; you can simplify the process while at the same time improving results. Often managers who dread review time have lost sight of the relationship between managing their team on a day-to-day basis and holding review meetings. While there are a number of ways to describe the purpose of review meetings, a simple definition is that a review meeting serves three functions:

1. To improve performance levels.

2. To manage individual behaviour.

3. To develop people.

1. IMPROVE PERFORMANCE LEVELS

Review meetings are essentially a platform to set goals to improve performance, "but goals don't float in space. They must be anchored in the bedrock of conviction, meaning, and purpose, because without this foundation of purpose, we're all too likely to throw our goals overboard at the first sign of adversity." (Vince Lombardi, 2000). The meeting is an opportunity to outline key priorities and expectation levels, and to align goals in a way that demonstrates their impact on the business strategy. In reality, a review meeting is formalising what you should be doing on a day-to-day basis with your team – managing their performance.

2. MANAGE INDIVIDUAL BEHAVIOUR

In addition to giving every goal a meaning, you must also outline how you want your team to achieve these goals. A regular complaint from managers is that individuals within their team lack drive, innovation and personal responsibility. A review meeting is a great opportunity to set down standards of behaviour and to instil a culture of responsibility and discipline. It reinforces the message about how you like things done in your team and how people should interact with each other.

3. DEVELOP PEOPLE

Upskilling your team is a constant requirement – you can't expect people to perform when goals regularly change to meet new demands while at the same time having a lack of training. As a leader you need to ensure that your team has the necessary skills, knowledge and expertise to do their work today and also to prepare them for the work of the future.

As a leader, you need to create an environment where the approach to performance review meetings is proactive and business-driven and where the focus is always on achieving high performance. Each individual needs to take responsibility for their performance and their strategy for achieving results. This may require a new way of thinking for some people.

Now is the time to make the change from the traditional, one-dimensional review meetings to the more dynamic PEAK Leadership approach. This approach transforms the way your people prepare for their meetings and how they participate in them. Moreover, it makes them more accountable for their performance. By implementing the principles of PEAK Leadership, you can transition from annual, appraisal-focused meetings to an ongoing, high-performance-driven process.

The heart of the PEAK Leadership approach is built around simple business planning principles. It focuses on good conversations, outlining goals and targets, providing a sense of direction and reviewing progress. Review meetings should be viewed as an extension of managing people on a day-to-day basis. The interaction in a review meeting should be no different from your daily interaction when dealing with performance issues, outlining key priorities for the week or giving praise for a job well done. Consider how you would use the PEAK Leadership model to integrate review meetings into your daily managerial responsibilities.

FIGURE 2.1 — PEAK LEADERSHIP

PERFORMANCE IS CHALLENGED

ENVIRONMENT IS CREATED

ALIGN THE GOALS

KEEP STAFF ENGAGED

PEAK Leadership – Performance is challenged

Challenging the performance of people isn't about simply saying "you got to do better". It's about establishing if there is a better way of doing things, if the performance can be improved and why it needs to be improved. It must be put into the context of the overall performance of the person.

Evaluating an individual's capacity for improvement starts with understanding a simple performance formula (see Figure 2.2) and how it impacts results. High performance is based on three interconnecting components: (1) the **ability** of your team plus (2) how they **execute** their tasks minus (3) any performance **blocks**. Each of these components alone is visible to managers, but many underestimate their importance and how they are connected. They focus their attention on improving the ability of their team while failing to accurately outline how they expect the team to execute their tasks. They also fail to adequately deal with any performance blocks. In some instances they may even unknowingly add more blocks through their own behaviour and negative mindset, for example by speaking negatively about review meetings or work colleagues.

FIGURE 2.2 — THE HIGH PERFORMANCE FORMULA

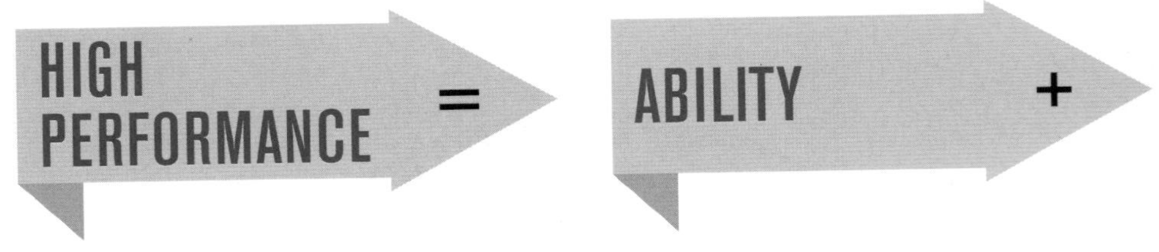

I developed this performance model to help you, as a manager, to focus on the actions you need to take to challenge the performance of your team. By evaluating each component, you can determine which areas require improvement and link your findings to your team's learning and development. At first, challenging performance should always focus on areas that can be improved and deliver best results. When you achieve quick wins and noticeable improvements, people are more inclined to look for additional ways to improve. Over time you can then raise the bar in more difficult areas.

ABILITY This is the skill, knowledge and expertise that each member of your team requires in order to achieve the results expected of them. Often you have hired people specifically because of their skills and experience to do a certain job. The question post-hiring then becomes: are those skills at the standard required to do the job as expected? Do they need further development? Has the job evolved over time but the person's skills haven't?

When you set goals and targets at review meetings, you need to ensure that the person has the ability to achieve the expected results – otherwise their performance will be adversely affected. Top sportspeople routinely work on improving their skills and techniques because they want to remain at the top; the same principles apply in the business world. Challenge people to continually evaluate and benchmark their skill levels against their peers, both internally and within their industry.

Sometimes people achieve their goals but their managers are ultimately unhappy with their performance – usually because of their approach.

"Alex was set a goal to reduce the cost of running the company's canteen by 15% by the end of the first quarter. He diligently went about achieving this goal and, to his manager's surprise, this was achieved by the end of the second month. Although the goal was completed, the fallout soon became evident. Alex's approach was less than diplomatic. She managed to sufficiently annoy their main supplier, by changing their credit terms without consultation (this was discovered later by their finance manager and was the final straw), that they cancelled the contract. While the new supplier was cheaper, the quality and reliability was inferior. As a result, most staff either complained or boycotted the canteen. Alex may argue that she achieved the goal, but her approach meant that the overall cost was high."

BLOCKS

EXECUTION This is how each member of your team uses their abilities (i.e. skills, knowledge and expertise) to achieve the desired results and reach their goals. There are two distinct factors that must be considered when setting a performance goal: the 'what' and 'how'. The conversation must always clearly outline what is the goal and how do you want your team to achieve their goals. Lack of clarity when discussing the "how" will result in misunderstanding around the execution of the goals. Managers must spend more time asking their team these questions: what is their understanding of each goal, what core competencies will they need and how will they approach their goals? The level of experience of each person will determine if the manager is spending more time guiding or supporting the person. New or inexperienced people will require more guidance in identifying the best approach for achieving their goals.

BLOCKS During review meetings most managers focus on the ability and execution components when it comes to discussing performance. They are generally comfortable explaining what needs to get done and how they would like their team to approach their work. However, there is a third component that is often overlooked. These are the blocks to high performance and as managers you must identify and remove them. Blocks are behaviours, attitudes or mindsets that prevent people from achieving their goals. Some are easy to identify while others sit bubbling under the surface. If left unchecked, they can cause serious damage to performance levels.

Although there are any number of blocks, Figure 2.3 shows some of the key ones to look out for.

FIGURE 2.3 — PERFORMANCE BLOCKS

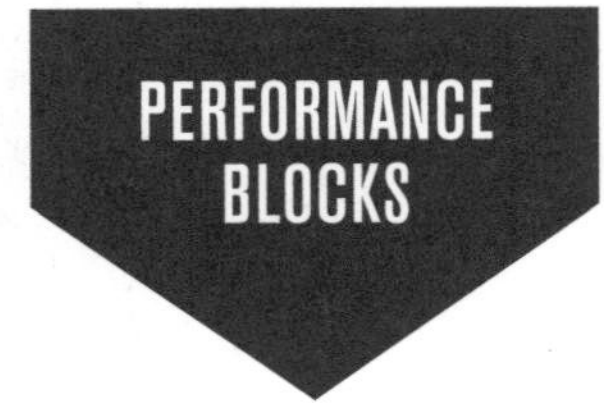

NEGATIVE EMPLOYEE MINDSET

CORE COMPETENCIES
DO NOT LINK WITH GOALS

APATHY TOWARDS REVIEW
MEETINGS AND GOAL SETTING

POOR TIME MANAGEMENT
AND PRIORITISING SKILLS

BLOCKS PUT THERE BY MANAGERS

DISCONNECT BETWEEN DAY-TO-DAY
JOB AND BUSINESS GOALS

LACK OF TRANSPARENCY
IN THE PERFORMANCE
MANAGEMENT PROCESS

Negative employee mindset

Don Keough wrote a great book about how to lose in business entitled *The Ten Commandments for Business Failure*. Two of these commandments – "T-G-E: That's Good Enough" and "T-N-M-J: That's Not My Job!" – are particularly relevant to individual performance. Although most people won't utter the words "that's not my job", they will display it through their actions.

Removing the negative employee mindset can be a big challenge, especially if it has gone unchecked for some time. The problem with a negative employee mindset is that most people can see the characteristics in other people, but aren't sufficiently self-aware to see it in themselves. Therefore, they believe that they have none of the symptoms.

IT HAPPENS

During one of my workshops I was explaining the concept of negative employee mindset and how it impacts performance. I mentioned "That's Not My Job!" to the group and they immediately agreed with me. They proceeded to tell me a few stories about how rampant it was in their company and how it affected their performance. Indeed, many of their examples were serious. However, one example made me laugh because they didn't realise that they were displaying the symptoms we were discussing. They explained that one of their colleagues had recently joined their company and after six weeks he still hadn't received a copy of their catalogue and this was preventing him from selling as he had no price listing.

"How can he do his job, Sean?" they asked. My reply was straightforward:

"Do you all have a catalogue?"

There was a chorus of "yes" from the group.

"Do you have a photocopier?"

"Yes."

"Why can't one of you photocopy the catalogue for him, or why can't he photocopy it?"

"But that's not our job, his manager should have got him a catalogue from day one."

It took a minute or two of silence from me for the group to realise that they had just fallen foul of the T-N-M-J negative mindset.

Here are just some of the examples of the negative employee mindset that you need to identify and change.

FIGURE 2.4 — CHECKLIST FOR A NEGATIVE EMPLOYEE MINDSET

CHECKLIST FOR A NEGATIVE EMPLOYEE MINDSET	✓
"That's not my job"	
Clock-watchers	
Lack of suggestions or participation	
Constant negativity about the team and/or the company	
Lack of teamwork/team thinking	
No sense of ownership/ responsibility for tasks	
Badmouthing people or other departments	
'Silo mentality' and creating divisions within/between teams/ departments	
Poor communication with colleagues/manager	
Carrying around a lot of baggage/negative history	
Refusing to go the extra step for customers	
"I'm not paid to do this task – it's above my pay grade!"	
Lack of energy, enthusiasm and respect for others	
Only thinking of themselves	
Lack of interest in the job	
Sense of entitlement	
"Nobody told me to do it"	
"I get no thanks, so why should I?"	
Automatically complains about any changes	

Core competencies do not link with goals
Discussing core competencies without linking them to specific goals leads to confusion around the relevance of some competencies. Put simply, competencies are the behaviours required to perform a particular job, such as relationship building, communication skills, analytical thinking and professional judgement. The potential list is endless and should depend on the requirements for each role. Therefore, commenting on someone's presentation skills when their role doesn't require it simply adds to the disconnect between day-to-day activities and review meetings.

During an annual review meeting a manager spent on average 1 hour and 25 minutes discussing 35 core competencies with each member of her team. Each competency was ranked and a small comment added. At no stage during this part of the review were any of the competencies linked to a specific goal. As a result, neither the manager nor any of her team saw the relevance and merely treated it as a form-filling exercise.

Apathy towards review meetings and goal setting
In many cases managers and their teams see review meetings as a chore, something that isn't part of their normal job. There is a growing disconnect between review meetings and the day-to-day management of people. Both parties see performance management in operation only two or three times a year and they believe it to be a standalone event. It is rarely embedded in organisations as something that is a great tool for improving performance. The irony is that review meetings were introduced to help and support managers, but for many these feelings are a block to achieving results.

Poor time management and prioritising skills

Productivity can be improved even where the working environment is full of busy people. The challenge for managers isn't about keeping their teams busy, but keeping them busy doing the right things. A common block to high performance is the inability to plan and prioritise daily, weekly and monthly activities. This problem isn't helped when work is delegated without clarity and an open discussion around priority levels. As a result, people are more likely to organise their tasks based on urgency rather than importance. In addition, when goals are handed out during review meetings they are often seen as extra work rather than part of the job. This further confuses people when prioritising.

Blocks put there by managers

Managers can also be the source of performance blocks, particularly where review meetings are concerned. For example, a last-minute approach to organising review meetings, constant cancelling and rescheduling them and a lack of preparation. This approach sends a very negative message to the team. When a meeting is rescheduled a number of times, you are effectively telling the team that these meetings aren't important. Participation drops and they quickly turn into a "tell me what I have to do" session, and engagement is low.

Disconnect between day-to-day job and business goals

Aligning business goals to daily tasks is an important factor in securing buy-in from your team. However, in many meetings sufficient time or effort isn't spent on ensuring the clarity of goals and how they impact the bottom line. The business plan is rarely discussed and therefore there is little understanding of what the key priorities for the business are. A manager cannot assume all of his/her team knows how their day-to-day activities fit into the business strategy if the plan isn't fully explained.

The timetable for this company with a staff of 145 is completely out of alignment:

End of Jan.	– All staff reviews are to be completed
End of Feb.	– All manager reviews are to be completed
Mid-April	– The business plan is to be completed

Everyone's goals should be aligned to the business and cascade down from the business plan. In effect, all of your team should be helping you achieve your goals through their day-to-day activities.

Lack of transparency in the performance management process

Another common block is a lack of transparency in the process. This is evident when there is a breakdown in trust, for example where the review meeting is viewed as a way for the company to avoid paying bonuses or raise pay rather than as a way to communicate effectively. A lack of transparency could also occur where there is little effort to differentiate poor performers from top performers. In a misguided attempt to be liked, you give everyone the same score or rating. People are given these scores without understanding how you arrived at them, and will then believe that their efforts during the year are based on whether or not they are liked.

There is a reluctance by many managers to clearly explain the scoring methodology for each goal at the start of the year. They are unable to articulate how someone can exceed their goals and achieve a high score. The reason often cited by managers is that they don't want too many people exceeding their goals in case they can't reward them with a bonus. However, a scoring process that lacks transparency leaves them open to accusations that the scores are predetermined and the review meeting is pointless.

PEAK Leadership – environment is created

In most situations your team will be made up of talented people who are driven to succeed, as well as others who display a negative employee mindset. Creating the right environment will help you establish a high-performance culture for everyone on your team.

Leaders inspire by encouraging an environment of success. In the PEAK Leadership model, in order for you to challenge performance on a regular basis, you must create the right environment, otherwise it will be counterproductive; people will feel overworked and stressed. Research upon research has shown that most people are motivated by things other than money. Talented people need to know that their input has meaning and makes an impact. They require reassurances that their efforts are acknowledged and that they make a difference.

If they are not getting this from their manager, they will move elsewhere to find it. This turnover of talented staff should not come as a surprise as the main characteristics of successful people can be summarised as follows:

- They have a definite SMARTER goal (see page 54), purpose or vision, as success requires a concentrated effort. Successful people are focused on achieving specific goals that are well defined and written down. Their focus is on the end result.
- They are willing to work hard and create momentum. Success breeds success because it is contagious. Smile while you work and maintain your energy, drive and passion for delivering outstanding performance.
- They realise the power of expectation – successful people expect the best and they usually get it. Aim high and with purpose!

If you have talented people in your team, does your approach to their review meeting match their characteristics? Put simply, are you giving them the confidence that you can facilitate their ambitions? If not, the chances are you will lose them to someone who will.

Reducing the blocks

Building an environment of success begins with reducing the number of performance blocks within your team. First, identify which blocks are affecting your team and then eliminate the problem. For example, a negative employee mindset is a common block that must be addressed before it becomes a major problem. The best way to deal with it is to reduce the risk of it happening in the first place. This can be achieved by closing the engagement gap.

Close the engagement gap

Generally, if you have hired the right person for the right job, then they don't become disengaged overnight. It is a gradual decline in the working relationship, often prompted by the perceived breaking of an unwritten contract. There is the formal written contract that sets out the terms and conditions of employment, outlining particulars such as job title, nature of the work and rate of remuneration. But there is also the unwritten contract; this is the contract that is made between a manager and staff at one level and the employer and staff at another level. It works on the principle that people offer their skills, knowledge and expertise and in return they need clarity around what is expected from them, a clear understanding of their goals and support from their manager and employer.

The engagement gap happens where there is an imbalance between staff needs and what the employer/manager offers. This leads to a reduction in performance and a negative employee mindset. On the flipside, an imbalance between the employer/manager needs and what staff offers leads to an expectation gap. This also leads to a reduction in performance because staff will spend too much time on lower-priority activities.

A simple methodology to establish if there is an engagement or expectation gap is to carry out a needs/offers analysis with your team. Use the framework shown in Figure 2.5 to start the conversation.

This exercise is simple to set up. Divide the flipchart into four squares as per Figure 2.5 and label them. Now ask the group to list everything that a company needs from its staff. Don't discuss anything on the list at this stage. Next, ask them to write down everything that staff need from their company. Again, don't discuss the list at this stage of the exercise. When this list is completed, write everything that staff offer their company on the flipchart. Finally, write down everything that a company offers its staff. This could take about 15 minutes. Encourage people to participate so that they will connect with the words on the flipcharts. At the end of the exercise you will end up with a list something like the one shown in Figure 2.6.

You now have a collection of data that needs to be explored. First, ask the participants to identify matching words in the opposite lists, "I Offer" and "Company Needs". While the words may match, their meanings will differ. To dig deeper, ask them to explain what they mean by each term under the heading "I Offer". For example, explore their understanding of flexibility and ask for some tangible examples.

Now change the "Company Needs" heading to "Manager Needs" and use the same responses. Explain, with tangible examples, what you need as a manager when you are looking for flexibility. The difference between the two interpretations of flexibility is the expectation gap. Repeat this exercise for some other key responses and you will build a picture of the full expectation gap between you and your team.

Now start with the "I Need" list. Again, look for the real meaning of each term. Then explain the "Company Offers" list. The different interpretations here will explain the engagement gap. This valuable information will allow you to take some remedial action.

The combined approach of reducing both the engagement gap and the expectation gap will produce better results than trying to close each gap separately. For best results, first close the engagement gap and then focus on closing the expectation gap. Research shows that engaged workers are more likely to achieve their goals. In a 2011 report carried out by the Aberdeen Group, Mollie Lombardi found that "in the top 20% of organizations, Aberdeen's Best-in-Class, 62% of employees rated themselves 'highly engaged' in their most recent engagement survey."

FIGURE 2.5 — NEEDS/OFFERS ANALYSIS

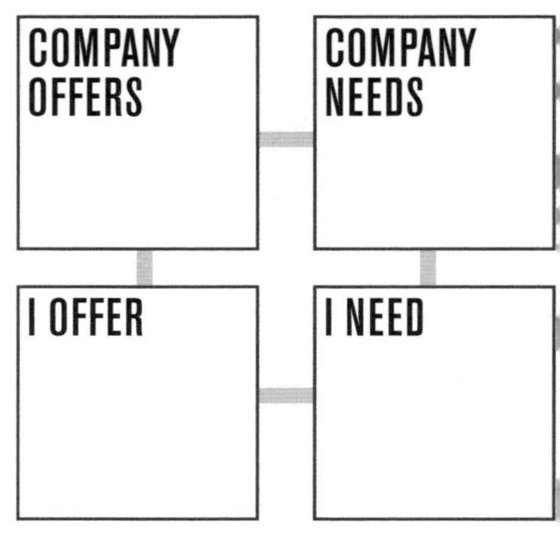

FIGURE 2.6 — COMPLETED NEEDS/OFFERS ANALYSIS

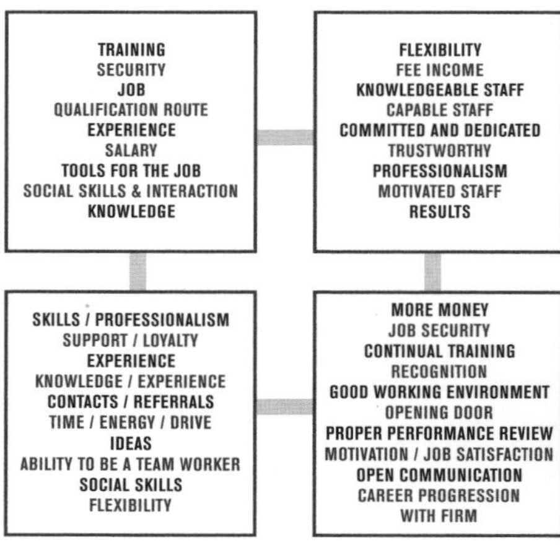

PEAK Leadership – Align the goals

Communication plays a pivotal role in reducing the expectation gap. By aligning all goals discussed during a review meeting with the organisation's business plan, you can steer the conversation towards your expectations levels. Discussing goals in isolation will create uncertainty around priorities.

Begin the conversation by highlighting the key business focus for the first quarter. For example, one of the business goals is to grow the new customer base by 15%. Although this goal is a priority for the sales team and you may work in the finance team, this goal is still a priority for your team. Therefore your conversation must move towards discussing how the finance team's goals are aligned to the growth of the customer base by 15%. For example, some of the goals that should emerge will concentrate on new reports for the marketing and sales teams, how to track and measure their leads, conversion rates and which channels are performing best. These goals are now aligned to the key business priority for first quarter.

PEAK Leadership – Keep staff engaged

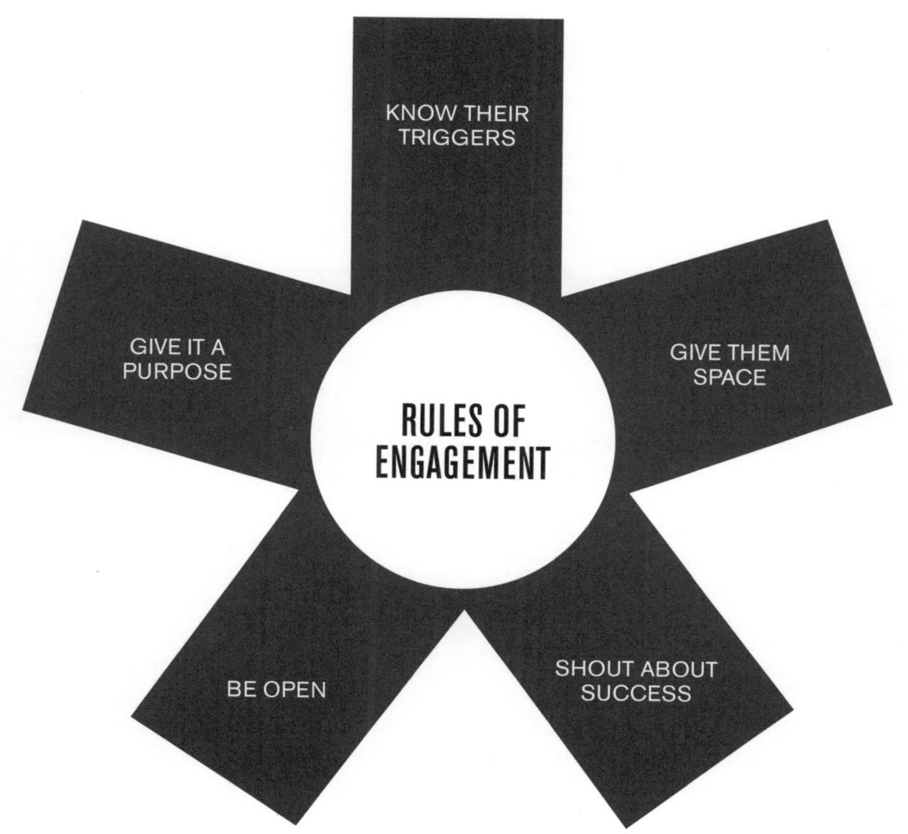

FIGURE 2.7 — FIVE RULES OF ENGAGEMENT

Five rules for keeping your team engaged

Once you have closed the engagement gap, you need to anchor this change by keeping your team engaged. There are five simple rules for maintaining a culture of engagement.

1. GIVE IT A PURPOSE Talented people need to feel part of something more important than just a job and a monthly pay cheque. Create a sense of purpose around everything that they do. Real meaning drives a higher level of performance because people can clearly see that their efforts count. Regularly explain how their role fits into the business and how they, as individuals, are impacting results.

2. KNOW THEIR TRIGGERS Connect with your team and understand their motivational triggers. Get to know and understand them as individuals. Find out what drives them, what's unique about them, what they value most about working for you and the company, how they work best, what their aims and career ambitions are. Figure out how they like to be managed and what's the best way to communicate with them. Once you understand your people, it will be easier to engage them.

3. GIVE THEM SPACE Give staff the space to grow and develop as people; discuss their personal learning and development plan and career path. Encourage them to try new ideas and to take the lead in an upcoming project. Create a culture where mistakes are tolerated and learned from. Set expectation levels and give them the scope to take responsibility for their performance.

4. BE OPEN AND HONEST Transparency is vital; ensure that there are no secrets or hidden agendas. You need to build trust with your team. Be upfront with information, particularly when it affects them. Discuss the business plan and its relevance to the team. Build the confidence within your team that you have the ability and expertise to lead them to success.

5. SHOUT ABOUT THEIR SUCCESSES Recognise your top performers and heap praise on them. If you regularly fail to recognise great performance, then don't be surprised when it isn't repeated. Making a big deal of your team's achievements, both individually and as a team, ensures their successes will be multiplied. Link their success to the impact on the business and comment on individuals' contributions.

AT A GLANCE — CHAPTER TWO

It's time to question the logic of once-a-year appraisals.

Would you run a business without a business plan? Or turn up at a meeting with your most important customer with little or no preparation?

Start using the PEAK Leadership approach for your review meetings.

The heart of the PEAK Leadership approach is that you and your team understand that review meetings are a normal part of the experience of managing people on a day-to-day basis. Keep in mind that your review meetings should improve performance levels, help to manage individual behaviours and develop the talent within your team

The interaction in a review meeting should be no different from your daily interaction when dealing with performance issues, outlining key priorities for the week or giving praise for a job well done.

Use the performance formula to identify problem areas:

High performance = Ability + Execution – Blocks

Consider how you would use the PEAK Leadership model to connect review meetings with your daily managerial role.

- Performance is challenged by removing blocks (e.g. negative employee mindset).
- Environment is created by ensuring the fulfilment of the unwritten contract (e.g. by using a needs/offers analysis).
- Align the goals through two-way communication.
- Keep staff engaged with the five rules of engagement.

CHAPTER THREE

PREPARE TO PREPARE

IT HAPPENS

"Alex, what time is your review meeting today? I forgot to put it in my diary. Can you also get HR to send me a copy of last year's report? I suppose I should have a quick look at it before I appraise you. Bring some coffees with you as well, I need something strong to get me through the meeting."

Are you ready for the performance review meetings?

Before you begin conducting performance review meetings, there are a number of activities you must complete in order to ensure their success. As the team leader, you will set the tone for what happens before, during (see **Chapter** 4) and after (see **Chapter** 7) each meeting. Applying some simple 'business planning' principles to your meetings starts with your preparation. Create a one-page roadmap for all the activities that you need to do. This roadmap benefits both you and your team as it focuses everyone's attention on the upcoming performance review meetings in their entirety. It should outline timelines for each activity and assigned responsibilities. This means you must have a clear understanding of all the activities required.

These meetings depend on the participation of multiple people, so this roadmap will make sure that everyone involved understands their responsibilities and timelines. There are a number of key elements that should be included in your road map (see Figure 3.1).

Investing some time in developing this roadmap means that you will have to spend less time preparing for subsequent meetings. Building a bank of good questions to ask, designing checklists and thinking about the logistics for each meeting will not only enhance their quality and content but can be used repeatedly.

FIGURE 3.1 — ROADMAP FOR REVIEW MEETINGS

SECTION	WHO	BY WHEN
Key success indicators		
Preliminary briefing		
Checklists		
Discuss the business plan		
Questions to ask		
Core competencies		
Preparation guide – pre-assessment forms		
Logistics		
Proposed schedule		

Key success indicators

This section of your roadmap provides you with a clear description of what success looks like for each person on your team. It answers the question, "A year from now, what does this person need to have done/accomplished in order to be considered a great performer in their role?" This information helps you and your team to set SMARTER goals (see page 54) based on your expectations of their performance. It is much broader than a simple job description; it outlines what success looks like in their roles. It is the 'what you want to be done' and 'how you want it to be done' summary for each role.

Defining what success looks like for each role can be difficult and as a result many people don't invest the time in writing clear success indicators. There is often an 'I know it when I see it' mentality or a belief that it takes too much time to write clear goals. To overcome this block, start with some questions about how each person can help you achieve your business goals.

- What needs to happen for my team to spend 70% of their time working on achieving my top business priorities?
- How can I get my team to fully understand what success looks like and what is expected of them?
- What if my team set their own goals that were aligned to my goals and then exceed my expectations?

Begin the process of composing the team's success indicators by writing some bullet points highlighting what they need to achieve. This will give you a high-level overview that details what you expect of each person for their specific rank. For instance, what would you expect a trainee to do to ensure that your business goals are achieved?

Now you should record the output from this exercise in a simple performance summary document (see Figure 3.2). This document highlights what success looks like for each person on your team. It is a quick way to ensure that all individual goals are aligned to the business goals and a helpful guide during the review meetings.

FIGURE 3.2 — PERFORMANCE SUMMARY DOCUMENT

PERFORMANCE INDICATORS

BUSINESS GOAL

Reduce by 5% the costs of running the business by the end of the first quarter.

SUCCESS INDICATORS FOR ALEX

Has taken on the role of looking after the stationery within the department. Has reviewed how much is spent on stationery by our department and identified areas of spending that could be cut without impacting negatively on the department. Has collaborated successfully with all stakeholders and has introduced a new ordering process that ensures we have enough stationery at all times while driving down costs through avoidable wastage. Has negotiated new terms with a supplier that can maintain the quality required and also within budget. Has successfully reduced costs by 28% by the end of Q1.

Preliminary briefing

The preliminary briefing is a short meeting that should last around 15 to 20 minutes. It is held a couple of weeks before the first review meetings of the year. During this briefing you will discuss a few key points, including those outlined in Figure 3.3.

FIGURE 3.3 — AGENDA FOR PRELIMINARY MEETING

PURPOSE OF THE REVIEW MEETING

It is important to emphasise the benefits of the review meetings to your team from their perspective. This is the beginning of building a high-performance culture within your team. Discussing this prior to the meeting itself ensures that everyone is focused on their performance and what they need to do for the next review period.

EACH PERSON'S ROLE AND RESPONSIBILITIES REGARDING THE REVIEW

Ensure that everyone is clear that this is their review and they are responsible for their performance. This means that they have a role to play in the process and they need to prepare fully for their review meeting.

REVIEW THE CHECKLISTS

To help them fully prepare for their meeting, quickly review the checklists and answer any questions the checklists might highlight.

DISCUSS THE REVIEW FORMS

Walk through the review documents and clarify any issues that your team may have with the forms. Discuss any changes to the previous forms. Again, emphasise that the forms are used to record what takes place at the meeting and should not be used to run the meeting. It is not a form-filling exercise.

THE TIMELINES AND DATE

Agree the timelines and emphasise the importance of not cancelling or rescheduling any meetings. The review meetings must be a priority for everyone.

At the end of the briefing, everyone involved should have a clear understanding of the purpose of the review meeting, the structure and what they need to do to fully prepare and engage in the process. For the subsequent quarterly review meetings, this preliminary briefing could be reduced to a quick five-minute session that could take place during your normal weekly team briefing.

Preparation guides

Pre-assessment or self-appraisal forms are often used as a way to ensure that everyone is fully prepared for their review meeting. It is usually a simple form that invites the employee to comment on their performance during the review period.

This form is completed prior to the meeting and is passed on to the manager at least a week before the meeting.

These forms can be helpful if you only have annual reviews and performance discussions aren't held regularly. They typically contain the details set out in Figure 3.4.

FIGURE 3.4 — PRE-REVIEW FORM

NAME	DEPARTMENT
	DATE
List your major achievements	1. 2. 3.
What was your biggest challenge?	
What additional topics would you like to discuss?	1. 2. 3.
What can your manager do differently to support you during the next review period?	
What training needs do you have?	

Checklists

Atul Gawande, a Boston general surgeon and author of *The Checklist Manifesto*, argues that we should "take a leaf from the commercial aviation industry and develop checklists that people can use to make sure every base is covered quickly and concisely." Developing a good preparation checklist for review meetings will save you time and keep you focused on the key steps. It also demonstrates the level of importance that you attach to these meetings.

The below list can be tailored to meet your specific requirements. During the debrief session after all the review meetings (see **Chapter 7**) are completed, you should update your checklist based on what you have learned.

FIGURE 3.5 — REVIEW MEETING PREPARATION CHECKLIST

ITEM	WHO	BY WHEN
Business plan signed-off		
Preliminary meeting set up		
Forms distributed		
Review meeting scheduled		
Rooms booked		
Personal business plans reviewed by both parties		
Coaching/training log reviewed by both parties		
Agenda for meeting completed and distributed		
Questions likely to be asked distributed to everyone		
Preparation guide – pre-assessment forms distributed		
All meetings completed		
Personal learning and development plans updated and copied to relevant people		
Documentation completed and returned to HR		
Update coaching/training plan for team		
Team debrief meeting scheduled		
Follow-up action plans distributed		

Discuss the business plan

An area that is often overlooked is discussing the company's business plan with your team prior to their review meetings. During this team meeting you should outline the key points of the plan and how it impacts the team. This will allow your team to figure out how they will contribute to successfully completing the goals of the plan. It will also ensure that their individual goals are aligned to your company's business goals.

This meeting should last about 90 minutes and is held prior to the first reviews of the business year. Initially, the input from the team can be very minimal. If you are persistent, however, the team will start to contribute to the discussion and the ideas will flow.

Start by outlining the organisation's high-level business plan. This will give the team a better understanding of how their role impacts the overall performance of the business. It will give their job a sense of purpose and belonging to something important. Then outline the priority areas for the team and outline your success indicators summary document. List these priorities on a flipchart.

Next, open the discussion by asking the team what they believe needs to happen in order to achieve the expected results. Facilitate this part of the meeting by encouraging each team member to contribute at least one idea. Again, list the ideas on the flipchart. The final piece of the process is to connect the success indicators to the list of ideas on the flipchart. Prioritise the ideas that are closest to the success indicator. This process will allow your team to plan their goals more effectively. Close the meeting by promising to distribute the outputs from the meeting within 24 hours. Encourage everyone to reflect on the meeting and start to figure out how they will contribute on an individual basis.

Once you have completed this exercise, you can start to write some SMARTER goals. It's always a good idea to write some sample goals prior to the review meeting so that you have something on which to base your conversations. It is easier to clarify performance expectations when you and your team collaborate in writing SMARTER goals. This can be done during the review meeting (see **chapter 4**). You can also discuss examples of tangible evidence that you will look for during the review period to confirm that they have achieved their goals.

Update your performance summary document with some sample SMARTER goals.

FIGURE 3.6 — UPDATED PERFORMANCE SUMMARY DOCUMENT

PERFORMANCE INDICATORS

BUSINESS GOAL

Reduce by 5% the costs of running the business by the end of the first quarter.

SUCCESS INDICATORS FOR ALEX

Has taken on the role of looking after the stationery within the department. Has reviewed how much is spent on stationery by our department and identified areas of spending that could be cut without impacting negatively on the department. Has collaborated successfully with all stakeholders and has introduced a new ordering process that ensures we have enough stationery at all times while driving down costs through avoidable wastage. Has negotiated new terms with a supplier that can maintain the quality required and also within budget. Has successfully reduced costs by 28% by the end of Q1.

SMARTER GOAL

Reduced the cost of stationery within the finance department by 28% by the end of Q1.

Prepare some questions for the review meeting

Most people are nervous about attending review meetings. They are unsure of what to expect or what they will be asked. You can reduce some of the anxiety by giving your team a checklist of the type of questions that you will use during the meeting. These questions need to be transparent because you don't want to engage in a practice of trying to catch people out. You will achieve a better summary of their performance if they are relaxed and fully prepared.

Since one of the objectives of a review meeting is to ensure full participation from your team, it is important that you have a range of thoughtful, open and probing questions that will encourage a productive conversation. Open questions start with "Kipling's 'six serving-men':

FIGURE 3.7 — SUGGESTED OPEN QUESTIONS FOR REVIEW MEETINGS

OPEN QUESTIONS

TEAMWORK
- How will you help build the culture within the team?
- How did you improve the team's performance this year?
- How have you added value to your team?
- In what way did you support your colleagues?
- How did you contribute to the team's success?

EXCEEDING EXPECTATIONS
- When did you exceed expectations in terms of performance?
- How will you exceed your business goals during the next review period?
- What are my (as manager) key priorities for this review period?

ADDING VALUE
- What would you like to achieve this year in addition to your business goals?
- How will you achieve this goal?
- How will it add value to the business and/or team?

CHALLENGES FOR THIS YEAR
- What would prevent you from achieving your goals in the next period?
- What support/assistance would you like/expect from me to help you achieve your goals?
- What is your biggest challenge this year?

IMPROVEMENT
- If there's one thing you could change about your performance last year, what would it be?
- What did you learn from this experience?
- What's your strategy to ensure it won't happen again this year?

What, Why, When, How, Where and Who, in no particular order" (Prone and Lyons, 2006). You can group a series of questions under various headings that you would like to cover, such as performance during the review period, personal development and how they liked to be managed.

Probing questions are useful to maintain the flow of the conversation. They help you dig deeper and explore further. However, be careful how you word these questions so that they don't appear to doubt responses. Use phrases such as, "Tell me more about how you went about..." and "I'm really interested in ... can you me tell your thought process for that decision?"

Figure 3.7 provides a list of open questions that you can use in most business review meetings.

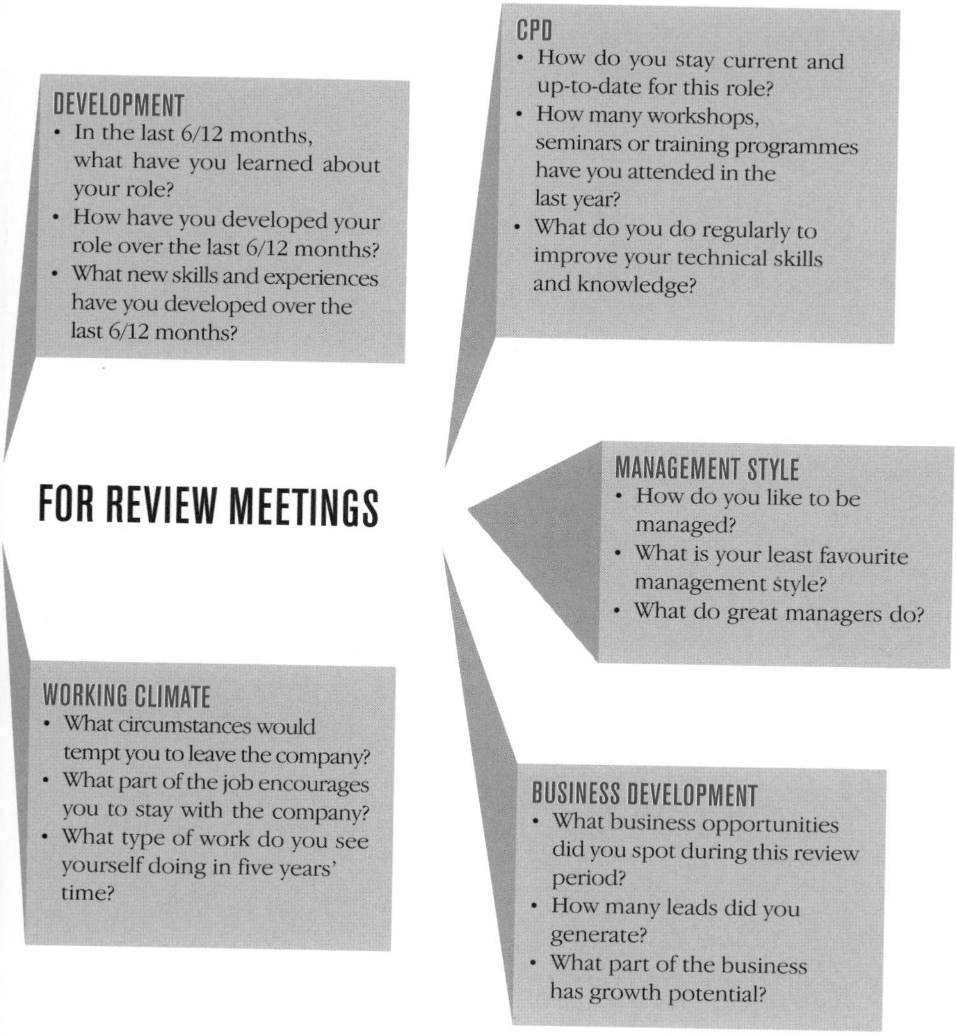

FOR REVIEW MEETINGS

DEVELOPMENT

- In the last 6/12 months, what have you learned about your role?
- How have you developed your role over the last 6/12 months?
- What new skills and experiences have you developed over the last 6/12 months?

CPD

- How do you stay current and up-to-date for this role?
- How many workshops, seminars or training programmes have you attended in the last year?
- What do you do regularly to improve your technical skills and knowledge?

MANAGEMENT STYLE

- How do you like to be managed?
- What is your least favourite management style?
- What do great managers do?

WORKING CLIMATE

- What circumstances would tempt you to leave the company?
- What part of the job encourages you to stay with the company?
- What type of work do you see yourself doing in five years' time?

BUSINESS DEVELOPMENT

- What business opportunities did you spot during this review period?
- How many leads did you generate?
- What part of the business has growth potential?

Every question you ask must have a purpose, so assess each question before your next meeting. Check with a colleague to see if the questions actually achieve their intended purpose. Every question that you use will determine the success of the meeting and quality of the information that you record about each individual. Figure 3.8 gives a list of dos and don'ts for writing good questions.

FIGURE 3.8 — THE DOS AND DON'TS OF ASKING GOOD QUESTIONS

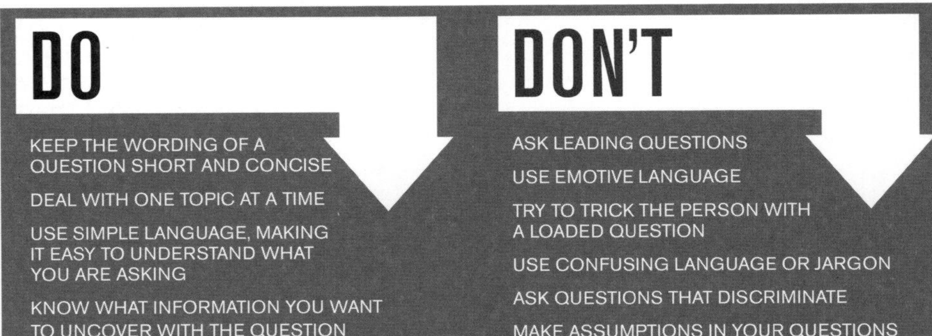

DO
KEEP THE WORDING OF A QUESTION SHORT AND CONCISE
DEAL WITH ONE TOPIC AT A TIME
USE SIMPLE LANGUAGE, MAKING IT EASY TO UNDERSTAND WHAT YOU ARE ASKING
KNOW WHAT INFORMATION YOU WANT TO UNCOVER WITH THE QUESTION
DON'T
ASK LEADING QUESTIONS
USE EMOTIVE LANGUAGE
TRY TO TRICK THE PERSON WITH A LOADED QUESTION
USE CONFUSING LANGUAGE OR JARGON
ASK QUESTIONS THAT DISCRIMINATE
MAKE ASSUMPTIONS IN YOUR QUESTIONS

Core competencies

Competencies are "the type of behaviour required to deliver results" (Armstrong, 2009). They are often grouped together in clusters according to the role or type of work that an individual performs. Figure 3.9 provides a list of common competencies and a short definition of each.

Some organisations will have a list of 30–40 competencies for each individual and will discuss each

FIGURE 3.9 — COMPETENCIES THAT CAN BE LINKED TO SUCCESS INDICATORS

ATTENTION TO DETAIL
Understanding the importance of presenting work in a professional manner.

ADAPTING TO CHANGE
Supporting opportunities for positive change and willingly helping others adapt to change.

BUILDING RELATIONSHIPS
Taking responsibility to build and maintain relationships with others that will add value to the team.

COMPLIANCE WITH POLICIES, PROCESSES AND PROCEDURES
Working within agreed guidelines at all times.

COMMITMENT TO THE TASK
Dedication to excellence and being prepared to put in the hours in order to get the job done.

CONTINUOUS LEARNING
Demonstrating a willingness to acquire the necessary skills, knowledge and expertise to achieve all current and future business goals.

COPING SKILLS
Coping well with demanding and strict deadlines. Keeping a cool head under pressure.

CUSTOMER FOCUS (EXTERNAL/INTERNAL)
Listening and responding to customers' requirements within the agreed customer care charter.

DECISIVENESS
Coming to conclusions quickly and taking immediate action based on available information.

DRIVE FOR EXCELLENCE
Showing a desire to consistently exceed expectations.

FLEXIBILITY AND VERSATILITY
Can perform a wide variety of tasks and has the ability to move from one task to another without compromising on quality.

INFLUENCE AND PERSUASION
Can positively influence to change others' behaviour, attitudes or beliefs.

INITIATIVE
Seeks out tasks that haven't been requested, looks for ways to improve the team's service or product.

INNOVATION
Thinking outside of comfort zone and looking at problems as a way of improving.

INTEGRITY
Holding oneself accountable for one's actions.

JUDGEMENT AND DECISION MAKING
Making decisions within authority level and considering all available courses of action before deciding on the best option.

one during the review meeting. This can be very cumbersome and time consuming, as the individual has to think of 30–40 examples of how they demonstrated these competencies. However, it is essential that competencies are discussed because they affect overall performance.

Organisations that are successful in using competencies to help improve performance will focus on a small group of core competencies for each role. They will identify key behaviours for each person and discuss them during the meeting (**Chapter 4** explains how to combine a goal with a competency). The difficulty here is linking the list of competencies to the business objectives. Before each meeting, decide which competencies are most closely linked to the overall business plan and their success indicators.

Include these core competencies when you write your performance summary document. The performance summary highlights what success looks like for each person on your team. It is a quick way to ensure that all individual goals are aligned to the business goals and that the core competencies are linked to these goals (see Figures 3.9 and 3.10).

MANAGING CONFLICT
Dealing with conflict in a way that allows all parties to move forward.

NEGOTIATING
Reaching mutually accepted agreements.

PLANNING, PRIORITISING AND GOAL SETTING
Adopting a structured approach to achieving key priorities on a daily, monthly and yearly basis.

PROFESSIONAL / TECHNICAL KNOWLEDGE
Demonstrating competent professional/technical knowledge of one's job, procedures, processes and relevant technology.

QUALITY AND CONSISTENCY OF WORK
Demonstrating an ability to maintain a high level of performance within the constraints of the job.

RESPECTING AND SUPPORTING DIVERSITY
Supporting the diversity policy within the company through actions and respect for colleagues.

TEAM WORK AND COOPERATION
Demonstrating an ability to work harmoniously with colleagues, management and peers.

CLEAR COMMUNICATION
Communicating in a way that is readily understood.

FIGURE 3.10 — UPDATED PERFORMANCE SUMMARY DOCUMENT

PERFORMANCE INDICATORS

BUSINESS GOAL

Reduce by 5% the costs of running the business by the end of the first quarter.

SUCCESS INDICATORS FOR ALEX

Has taken on the role of looking after the stationery within the department. Has reviewed how much is spent on stationery by our department and identified areas of spending that could be cut without impacting negatively on the department. Has collaborated successfully with all stakeholders and has introduced a new ordering process that ensures we have enough stationery at all times while driving down costs through avoidable wastage. Has negotiated new terms with a supplier that can maintain the quality required and also within budget. Has successfully reduced costs by 28% by the end of Q1.

SMARTER GOAL

Reduced the cost of stationery within the finance department by 28% by the end of Q1.

CORE COMPETENCY

Use of influencing, negotiation and collaboration skills.

Preparation guides

Another set of forms that needs to be renamed and revamped are the pre-assessment forms. Simply call them the 'preparation guides'. Keep this form short and easy to complete. The purpose of the preparation guide is to remind people of the areas to concentrate on in their preparation for their review. It should be filled out after the business plan meeting.

FIGURE 3.11 — PREPARATION GUIDE TEMPLATE

BUSINESS GOAL

NAME	DEPARTMENT	DATE

Success indicators for last period	SMARTER goal and tangible evidence for last period
1.	1.
2.	2.
3.	3.
Success indicators for next period	**SMARTER goal to achieve for next period**
1.	1.
2.	2.
3.	3.

Personal learning and development plan

Additional topics for agenda

SIGNED:	DATE:

This guide will help your team prepare for their meeting by gathering tangible evidence to support their assessment of their performance. It moves the conversation from a subjective point of view to a more results-focused conversation. This form should relate back to the SMARTER goals set at their last review meeting.

FIGURE 3.12 — PROPOSED SCHEDULE OF EVENTS

ACTIVITY	OWNER	ESTIMATED TIME TO COMPLETE	DUE DATE	STATUS
Business plan written	Senior management	One month	Third week in Nov.	
Success indicators	Manager	One day	Second week in Dec.	
Preliminary meeting	Manager	Three hours	Third week in Nov.	
Checklist updated	Senior member of team	One hour	Third week in Nov.	
Business plan discussion meeting	Manager	One day	First week in Dec.	
Preparation for actual meeting, SMARTER goals, PBP plan	Everyone on the team	Two days	Third week in Dec.	
Review meeting	Everyone on the team	One hour per person	First & second weeks in Jan.	
Debrief after meetings	Everyone on the team	Two hours	First week in Feb.	

Planning the logistics for your meetings

Creating the right atmosphere for a productive review begins with the logistics. "Even the simple things (like the venue) have a real impact on how motivational the meeting is" (Henshaw, 2013), so it's worth spending some time on ensuring that you get the logistics right. There are three key areas to focus on: timings, venue and documentation.

Agree a specific time with everyone on your team and confirm it in writing. If you have a team calendar, make sure these meetings are diarized. Never cancel or change these times as it sends out the wrong message; careful planning should ensure that there are no acceptable reasons for cancelling. Once you have agreed the time, work back and start to allocate sufficient time for preparation (e.g. around two to three weeks' notice).

The venue is also important. Book a neutral room (not your office) if possible. If you have no meeting rooms, buddy up with another manager and swap offices. Ensure that the room is quiet and that there are no interruptions, turn off all phones and computers, and have some water or coffee/tea available.

Check that you have all the necessary and up-to-date documentation or login codes for the meeting. If there were any changes to the forms or structure from the previous year, make sure you understand how to complete the new forms. If you are using an online version, ensure you fully understand how to navigate your way through it. Read all guidelines and policy documents before the meeting and ensure your team understands how to complete all documentation.

Proposed schedule

It is common for both managers and their teams to underestimate the amount of time required to adequately prepare for the first review meeting of the year. By drafting a simple schedule of events with dates and time frames, you can help your team prepare effectively for their meeting (see Figure 3.12 on page 41). Reassess this schedule at regular intervals and make adjustments to ensure the meetings take place at the agreed times.

AT A GLANCE — CHAPTER THREE

Applying some simple 'Business Planning' principles to your meetings starts with your preparation. Create a one-page roadmap for all the activities you need to do.

Key success indicators provide you with a clear description of what success looks like for each person on your team.

The preliminary briefing lasts only around 15–20 minutes and should outline how to prepare for the upcoming review meetings.

Developing a checklist for business review meetings will save you time and keep you focused on the key steps.

Hold a meeting at the start of the year to discuss the company's business plan. This will allow your team to figure out how they can contribute to it. It will also ensure that their individual goals are aligned to your company's business goals.

Most people are nervous about their review meeting. You can reduce some of the anxiety by giving your team a checklist of the type of questions you will use during the meeting.

Help improve performance by focusing on a small group of core competencies for each role. Before each meeting, decide which competencies are most closely linked to the overall business plan.

The purpose of the preparation guide is to remind people of the areas to concentrate on in preparing for their review meeting.

Draft a simple schedule of events with dates and time frames; this will help your team prepare effectively for their meeting.

CHAPTER FOUR

HOLDING THE REVIEW MEETING

Manager: Alex, to be quite honest, I'm more than a little disappointed with your performance this year – you just haven't delivered.

Alex: This is the first I'm hearing of it, I think I had a great year. I introduced the new automated reporting system. They love it in accounts.

Manager: But Alex, that wasn't a priority for us. I needed you to help me drive down costs in production.

Alex: You never told me that I wasn't performing; you said I was to improve efficiencies. And I did. You can't turn around now and tell me I had a poor performance when I didn't.

Manager: I'm sorry, Alex, but you're going to get a 2.5 this year and no bonus.

Alex: You're kidding me…

Remember the purpose of the review meeting

Before launching into a series of review meetings, it's worth taking a step back and revisiting their key objectives. You want your team to leave their review meeting inspired to do great things, fully understanding what is expected of them and focused on contributing to the business plan. This is achieved by setting clear goals and giving regular feedback on these goals. The meeting should answer three simple questions:

- What level of performance do you expect from each person in their current role?
- How have they performed against this expectation during the previous period?
- What do they need to do for the next review period and how will you support them?

In answering these questions it is important that there are no surprises at any stage of the meeting. Whether it's good or bad, no one should find out anything about their performance for the first time during the meeting. The meeting is a summary of their performance for that period and a business plan for the next period. It's not a time for scoring points or settling old arguments.

Therefore, you should spend approximately 30% of your allotted time discussing the period under review and 70% of the time outlining the goals and expectations for the next period. Review meetings should be future-based; you can't change past performance, but you can use it to influence future performance.

Two-way conversation

The best meetings are focused on having a good conversation where both the manager and team member discuss performance expectations, key priorities and any performance blocks such as lack of training or cooperation from colleagues. They also include a discussion around the contribution made to the success of the team and areas for further development.

The conversation needs to go two ways and cover the key topics that affect performance. Both parties must listen actively, understanding what is being said and listening for what isn't being said.

The format and content of each meeting will vary, but using some thought-provoking questions like these (given to your team with their checklist, see **Chapter 3**) will help to initiate a flowing two-way conversation.

Use these questions as a way of having a meaningful conversation with your team. A well-thought-out question will enable you to keep the conversation flowing and focused on their key activities. Encourage them to use practical examples in their answers. Then probe to gain a better understanding of their performance.

FIGURE 4.1 — THOUGHT-PROVOKING QUESTIONS

QUESTION

What would you like to achieve this year in addition to your business goals?

How will you achieve it?

How will it add value to the business?

PURPOSE - Gaining clarity about how the team member believes they can add value to the business; spot gaps in the alignment of the business plan and individual plan; see how they believe they can exceed expectation levels; good indicator of strategic awareness.

QUESTION

If there is one thing you could change about your performance last year, what would it be?

What did you learn from this experience?

What's your strategy to ensure it won't happen again this year?

PURPOSE - Providing a good indicator of personal responsibility and ownership of continuous improvement.

QUESTION

How did you improve your team's performance this year?

In what ways did you support your colleagues?

PURPOSE - Assessing their understanding of what it means to be a team player and how they impact the development of the team.

FIGURE 4.1 CONT. — THOUGHT-PROVOKING QUESTIONS

QUESTION

What would prevent you from achieving your goals in the next period?

What support/ assistance would you like/expect from me to help you achieve your goals?

What is your biggest challenge this year?

PURPOSE - Identifying potential issues for the next period, their ability to work with their head up and forecast any potential problems. Assessing their ability to ask for help and guidance.

QUESTION

What have you learned about your role in the last 6/12 months?

How have you developed your role over the last 6/12 months?

What new skills and experiences have you developed over the last 6/12 months?

PURPOSE - Ensuring that there is a culture of continuous learning and that each team member is responsible for their own development. Identifying proactive learners within the team.

QUESTION

How do you like to be managed?

What circumstances would tempt you to leave our company?

What part of the job encourages you to stay with the company?

PURPOSE - Finding out if your managerial style matches your team's needs.

QUESTION

How do you stay current and up-to-date in your profession?

How many workshops, seminars or training programmes have you attended in the last year?

What do you do regularly to improve yourself?

PURPOSE – Aligning continuous personal development with the needs of your team; establishing who the proactive learners are.

QUESTION

What business opportunities did you spot this year?

What part of the business has growth potential?

PURPOSE – Assessing business awareness and the ability to keep one eye on the future.

QUESTION

Where did you exceed performance expectations?

How do you propose to exceed your business goals during the next review period?

What are my (as manager) key priorities this review period?

PURPOSE – Establishing who is going the extra yard, and who understands what adds value to the business and how your key priorities fit into the overall business plan.

The five phases of a review meeting

A meeting can last anything from 40 minutes to two hours, depending on how often you hold them. A productive meeting is conducted in five phases:

FIGURE 4.2 — THE FIVE PHASES OF THE REVIEW MEETING

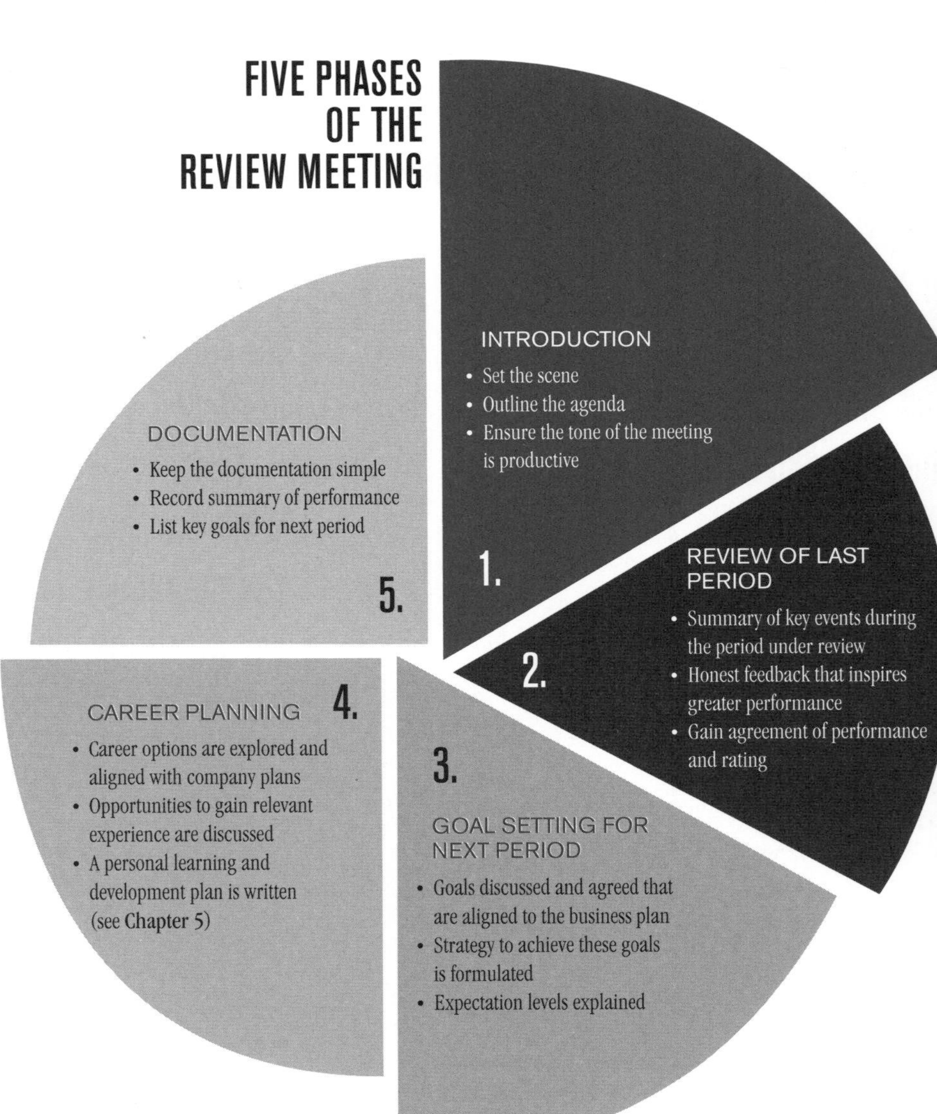

FIVE PHASES OF THE REVIEW MEETING
1.
INTRODUCTION
• Set the scene
• Outline the agenda
• Ensure the tone of the meeting is productive
2.
REVIEW OF LAST PERIOD
• Summary of key events during the period under review
• Honest feedback that inspires greater performance
• Gain agreement of performance and rating
3.
GOAL SETTING FOR NEXT PERIOD
• Goals discussed and agreed that are aligned to the business plan
• Strategy to achieve these goals is formulated
• Expectation levels explained
4.
CAREER PLANNING
• Career options are explored and aligned with company plans
• Opportunities to gain relevant experience are discussed
• A personal learning and development plan is written (see Chapter 5)
5.
DOCUMENTATION
• Keep the documentation simple
• Record summary of performance
• List key goals for next period

1. Introduction

BEGIN THE MEETING WITH A SMILE Ensuring that each team member is at ease is extremely important. You want them to interact with you in a productive way. Start the meeting by offering them a coffee, tea or water in the same way you would start a meeting with your most important client. Check that they have brought all of the necessary documentation and notes for the meeting. Quickly go through the agenda and ask if they are ready to proceed.

YOU CAN MAKE IT A POSITIVE MEETING, EVERY TIME As a leader, you set the tone for the conversation. It is worth remembering that if you don't bring energy to the meeting, if you're not excited and enthused about next year's plans or if you don't engage your team in a meaningful way, then you shouldn't expect great things from your team. They need to be reassured that this isn't a form-filling exercise or waste of their time.

If the preparation (including the business plan meeting) is completed successfully, then each team member should bring at least 50% of the goals to the meeting. Over time you can encourage people to set more business goals, and eventually you should be in a position where goals are set by each individual and you discuss their strategy to achieve them. When you get to this stage you will have a high-performing team inspired to achieve great things.

2. Review of last period

When you feel they are relaxed and ready for the meeting, outline the key goals you wish to discuss for the period under review. Invite them to summarise their performance for each goal and ensure they provide evidence to support their self-assessment. Use questions (see Figure 4.1) to probe further for more detailed information if necessary and take notes to aid clarity later. To verify that you understand what they have said, summarise their assessment in your own words.

Now give your assessment and feedback on their performance. Support your summary with specific and relevant examples. To help avoid confusion or misunderstanding later, it is a good practice for you to agree performance levels after discussing a goal before moving on to the next.

BUILD A FEEDBACK CULTURE One of the most difficult parts of the meeting is giving corrective feedback. Everyone says that they accept they need continuous feedback from their manager in order to improve their performance. However, in my experience, giving and receiving feedback isn't as easy as people think, especially if feedback isn't part of the culture of your team or organisation.

CRITICISM Vs FEEDBACK While feedback can be positive or negative, the unfortunate reality is that for most people feedback is usually associated with negativity. It comes in the form of criticism or throwaway comments like, "This report isn't good", "Your work is sloppy" or "Alex is much better than you". None of these statements is feedback and none is helpful.

Feedback is about improving performance, it's not an opportunity to beat someone up or blame someone for doing something wrong. A blame culture based on the past will not change the result. Consequently, feedback must be used to keep your team in the present and inspired to do great things. Dr Bob Rotella talks about the mental discipline of playing golf in the present: "To play golf as well as he can, a player has to focus his mind tightly on the shot he is playing now, in the present. If a golfer thinks about anything else, that pure reaction between eye and the brain and the nervous system is polluted. Performance usually suffers. This is just the way human beings are constructed." Feedback must focus on what you want the person to do and help to ensure that they take responsibility for achieving the desired results.

None of the feedback that you give during a meeting should come as a surprise. It should be consistent with the feedback that you gave throughout the year. In reality, it should simply be a summary.

WHY ARE MANAGERS RELUCTANT TO GIVE FEEDBACK? The lack of honest and regular feedback is a massive barrier to performance. If people don't know that they are underperforming or the negative impact that their behaviour has on the team, then it is unrealistic to expect them to change. Fear is often quoted as a reason why managers are reluctant to give feedback: fear that they could make the situation worse, fear that the employee might leave or fear that they might be not liked by the team.

FIGURE 4.3 — REASONS MANAGERS ARE RELUCTANT TO GIVE FEEDBACK

REASONS MANAGERS ARE RELUCTANT TO GIVE FEEDBACK
Lack of understanding of what feedback involves.
Afraid that they could make the situation worse.
Lack of awareness that someone needs feedback.
There is no feedback culture.
It is not seen as part of the manager's role.
Believes in a non-confrontational style of management.
Great feedback requires time and preparation.
The need to adapt their approach depending on the different personality types.

CONSEQUENCES OF POOR PERFORMANCE FEEDBACK Giving poor or no feedback can have a direct negative impact on performance and the team in general, as shown in Figure 4.4.

FIGURE 4.4 — THE CONSEQUENCES OF POOR FEEDBACK

CREATING A BLAME CULTURE INSTEAD OF A RESPONSIBILITY CULTURE.

DEMORALISING THE TEAM.

DAMAGING BOTH THE MANAGER'S AND INDIVIDUALS' CAREER PROGRESSION.

BEING SEEN TO REWARD POOR PERFORMANCE AND ACCEPT MEDIOCRITY.

CREATING A LACK OF ACCOUNTABILITY.

GIVING FEEDBACK USING THE BEST FEEDBACK FRAMEWORK Whether you are giving feedback during the meeting or during the normal working day, the principles are the same. The BEST feedback framework is designed to move from a blame culture to a responsibility culture, in which people are energised and enthusiastic about improving their performance.

The basic principles of feedback haven't changed in the last 30 years: ensure it is timely, fair and respectful. Always own the feedback; never dilute it by saying, "Head office is giving me a hard time over your performance, any chance you can improve?" It's your feedback, so own it throughout the conversation.

FIGURE 4.5 — THE BEST FEEDBACK FRAMEWORK

B	E	S	T
BEHAVIOUR & IMPACT	ESTABLISH CAUSE	SOLUTION / SUGGESTION	TIME

BEHAVIOUR AND IMPACT When a member of your team is underperforming, the first step is to sit down with them in a private area and discuss their performance. Outline their behaviour, not their personality or characteristics, and the impact that their behaviour has had on their performance or the performance of the team. Personally attacking someone isn't giving feedback and it is highly unlikely to improve performance. The person on the receiving end of this type of feedback will become defensive and stop listening. For example, if you receive a late report, refrain from giving feedback as in the following example:

IT HAPPENS Alex was talking to his colleague in an open-plan office when, from across the floor, his manager started to give him some loud feedback. The manager was returning from a meeting with a client that didn't go well and wasn't very pleased.

"Alex, this report is late as always. It's sloppy and full of errors. It's what I'd expect from a four-year-old. You're spending too much time organising your social life – you need to change your attitude or there's the door."

Deal with facts and examples when giving BEST feedback. It would have been better to sit Alex down in a private area or office, then take the emotions out of the conversation by summarising the specific facts. Once you have outlined the problem, you need to explain the impact that their behaviour has. Never assume that the person can make the connection between their behaviour and their performance. For example, you could approach the same situation as follows:

IT HAPPENS "Alex, I received your report at 3.00 today, which is 45 minutes late. I requested it to be ready at 2.15 because I had a meeting scheduled for 2.45 with the client. When I went looking for you, I was told you weren't back from lunch. The report also contains a number of spelling and grammar mistakes, five typos and three factually incorrect statements, including using 'gross margin' instead of 'net margin'. As a result I looked very unprofessional at the meeting. The client, who is one of our most important clients, wasn't happy and we had to reschedule the meeting for next week. As an experienced member of the team I would expect you to have had this report on my desk on time and free of errors. Why was the report late and how do you account for the mistakes?"

ESTABLISH THE ROOT CAUSE Once you have outlined the performance issue, stop and check that the person understands and agrees with your assessment of the problem. It is easy to go off track in an unstructured conversation. Always deal with one problem at a time to avoid confusion or getting side-tracked.

Next, establish the root cause of the problem. A big mistake made by managers is assuming they know the reason why someone didn't perform as expected. Often these assumptions are based on the manager's bias towards the person.

Asking tough questions about underperformance can be difficult for some managers. Children are great at using the 'why' question; they keep asking 'why?' until they understand. Although this can be very annoying for adults, it does ensure clarity and understanding for the child. In the business world you must use the 'why' question to establish the root cause of underperformance; otherwise you could waste time fixing the wrong problem.

In the example above, for instance, you could continue the conversation as shown to the right.

By asking a number of 'why' questions, you can quickly unearth the real reason why a member of your team is underperforming. In this example, it wasn't because Alex was lazy or didn't care; she simply didn't prioritise correctly. You have now identified an area that Alex can develop, namely her prioritising skills.

SOLUTIONS The BEST feedback conversation can now move from identifying the problem to finding solutions. Because we want people to take responsibility for their performance, it is important that you don't provide them with a specific solution. They need to figure out the best solution for themselves as this will encourage personal development.

Ask about their strategy for improvement. Again, using simple open questions, such as "How will you ensure that this doesn't happen again?" or "How do you propose to deal with the problem?" will move the conversation along. The focus of the conversation is fully on the actions that they will take; your role is one of support, so use positive words.

In some cases the person may be unable to find a solution. Give them some time to think and then offer them some suggestions. Remember, you want them to take responsibility for their performance, so they need to choose which action is the best to take. By offering a couple of suggestions you are still getting them to decide on their next course of action.

TIME FRAME TO ASSESS IMPROVEMENT The final part of BEST feedback is agreeing a timeframe for improvement. Ensure the timeframe is realistic so that the person can implement their actions. Also identify if they require any training to help achieve the desired results. Monitor their progress during this time and offer support and encouragement. Maintain a positive focus throughout the BEST feedback conversation.

FIGURE 4.6 — CONSTRUCTIVE FEEDBACK

CONSTRUCTIVE FEEDBACK
Focus on behaviours.
Gather all the facts before the discussion.
Show the impact of behaviour on performance.
Listen for clues for poor performance.
Keep ownership of the feedback at all times.
Gain commitment for improvement.
Show your support throughout the process.
Stay focused on the problem under review.
Allow them to come up with their own solutions.
Ensure the person takes full responsibility for their performance.
Identify and agree any training requirements.

3. Setting the goals for the next period

SETTING GOALS THE SMARTER WAY Once you have finished discussing the period under review, you can move to the goal setting phase. This is a critical part of any review meeting. It is a powerful way to inspire your team to achieve outstanding results through clear goals and regular feedback. Over the last 50 years it has become a standard method of managing people's performance. However, some managers still struggle to link what takes place in the review meeting with the day-to-day activities of the team.

Locke and Latham write that, "goals have two main attributes, namely content and intensity". This means that each goal that you set your team must be specific and measurable as well as engaging, so that each individual is committed to the goal. They also found that "specific, difficult goals lead to higher performance than no goals [or] vague, abstract goals such as 'do your best'".

Setting goals the SMARTER way is a framework I developed over the last 10 years to ensure that each goal you set has clarity, is challenging and feeds into the business plan. When used correctly, it outlines the value of each goal, which in turn ensures a higher level of engagement. It can also be used as the basis for giving feedback.

FIGURE 4.7 — SETTING SMARTER GOALS

MEASURABLE

Make sure to include a way to measure the goal in order to track its progress and to know when it is achieved. Again, this helps to move away from the notion of "I know a good performance when I see it". Some goals are easy to quantify, such as "complete six financial reviews per month" or "reduce costs by 5% by the end of the first quarter". Others will require more thought. The key to writing a good goal is to ensure that both parties are agreed on how you will measure it.

SMA

SPECIFIC

Avoid ambiguity or vagueness when setting goals at all costs. Goals such as "be a better team player" or "improve customer service" are too subjective. Specific goals should focus on the result; what you want the person to achieve. Writing your 'success indicators' puts you in a stronger position to write specific goals. So instead of asking someone to "improve customer service", define what that actually means. For instance, set a goal to reduce the length of time in dealing with customer complaints from three to two days.

ALIGNED

All goals that are agreed with your team must be aligned to the overall business plan. This ensures that all the efforts of your team are pointed in the right direction. Translate the high-level strategic business goals into meaningful individual goals for each member of your team. This alignment will also help bring a greater value and purpose to each goal.

REALISTIC

Having high expectations of your team is great, but be very careful that you don't set unachievable goals. You want to stretch people, encourage them to reach their potential and thereby bring value to the business. If your team sees their goals as unfair or unrealistic, they will give up. Involving the team in goal setting will help you establish how they feel about the goals; you can then deal with their concerns as they surface during the process.

When the goal is very challenging, take time to explain how you will support them in achieving it. You may need to break it down into smaller, more manageable chunks designed to drive specific behaviours.

TIME FRAME

A realistic time frame for every goal must be agreed. This will allow you to benchmark progress against proposed deadlines. It also helps with scheduling different goals throughout the year. During each quarter it is important to focus everyone's efforts on a specific goal.

ENGAGING

Getting buy-in from your team is the most critical part of goal setting. Research over the years has overwhelmingly shown that engaged staff perform at a higher level. Spending some time on this part of the goal-setting process will clearly improve performance levels.

This principle brings a value and purpose to each role within your team. A team leader needs to outline the impact that each goal has on the business plan and ensure people are excited about their work. Get this part right and your team will bring more energy, enthusiasm, effort, enjoyment and efficiency to their role.

RTER

REWARD

The final principle is directly linked to engagement. It is about the 'what's in it for me?' question. The bigger the personal reward, the greater the chances are that your team will overcome obstacles and successfully complete all their goals. The reward doesn't have to be financial, but it must mean something to the individual.

Discuss the reward from the individual's perspective rather than from the organisation's. As a manager, you need to understand what motivates your team. Link the benefits to their motivational needs. For example, if one of your team is looking for a promotion, you can outline how each goal can improve their prospects. Refer to the Needs/Offers analysis you carried out in **Chapter 3** when thinking about this.

FIGURE 4.8 — THE SMARTER WAY GOAL SETTING SYSTEM

SPECIFIC
MEASURABLE
ALIGNED
REALISTIC
TIME FRAME
ENGAGING
REWARD

The SMARTER Way goal-setting system is based on the principles set out in Figure 4.8.

Every goal you set should be broken down into two parts: clarity and buy-in. While most people should be familiar with the 'SMART–' portion, it is the buy-in component that separates managers from great leaders. They engage their team to bring energy, enthusiasm, excitement, enjoyment and effort to their work. Great leaders find a way to personalise the reward for each goal so that their team is focused on the result. They create an '–ER' component that is so large, any obstacle that gets in the way of the goal is removed (see Figure 4.9).

TURN VAGUE GOALS INTO SMARTER GOALS

One of the most difficult tasks in writing quality goals is avoiding vagueness and ambiguity. It is critical to note that vague goals contribute to underperformance and a considerable amount of wasted time. Badly written goals are the result of poor preparation, lack of clarity around the business plan and a desire to get it over with. However, putting the SMARTER Way goal-setting system into practice is simple. For example, if one of your strategic business goals is to reduce costs by 5%, a SMARTER goal could read as follows:

FIGURE 4.9 — GOAL CLARITY AND BUY IN

CLARITY	**SMART** GOALS
BUY IN	**E**NGAGING AND **R**EWARDING (ADDING THE –ER THAT CREATS SMARTER GOALS)

FIGURE 4.10 — SMARTER GOAL SETTING: EXAMPLE

SPECIFIC	Reduce the cost of print stationery within each department.
MEASURABLE	by 28% across the organisation.
ALIGNED	Business target is a 5% reduction in costs overall.
REALISTIC	Printing costs overran last year by 12%, other alternatives to printing are available to the organisation.
TIME FRAME	By the end of Q1.
ENGAGING	Cross-departmental exposure, develop influencing skills, look for innovative ways to reduce printing costs.
REWARD	Improves profile; links to career path and promotional prospects.

GOAL SYNERGY In sport we are used to the term 'combination effect', when a coach combines two activities that, when done together, will multiply the benefit. Top sportspeople will do it to give themselves the edge; for instance, they will combine stamina training with a better diet, skills training and mental conditioning. More and more organisations are following their lead, visibly combining core competencies with business goals; in other cases they combine a business goal with a learning and development goal.

FIGURE 4.11 — COMBINING A BUSINESS GOAL WITH A CORE COMPETENCY

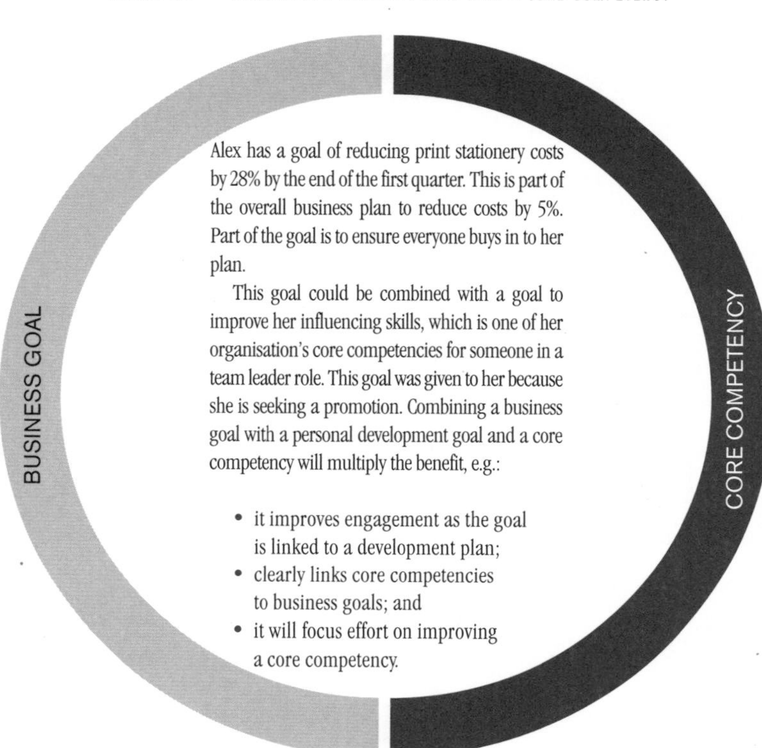

BUSINESS GOAL
CORE COMPETENCY
Alex has a goal of reducing print stationery costs by 28% by the end of the first quarter. This is part of the overall business plan to reduce costs by 5%. Part of the goal is to ensure everyone buys in to her plan.
This goal could be combined with a goal to improve her influencing skills, which is one of her organisation's core competencies for someone in a team leader role. This goal was given to her because she is seeking a promotion. Combining a business goal with a personal development goal and a core competency will multiply the benefit, e.g.:
• it improves engagement as the goal is linked to a development plan;
• clearly links core competencies to business goals; and
• it will focus effort on improving a core competency.

4. Career planning

TALENTS NEED TO BE MANAGED This part of the meeting is often overlooked. In many cases the manager will simply outline some routine training options that aren't aligned to career or team development; it's a box on the form that needs to be filled in. Expecting your team to grow and develop without your support is unrealistic. Your top talent need their careers to be managed effectively so that they will remain engaged and fulfil their potential. I will discuss career planning and development in more detail in **Chapter 5**.

5. Documentation

THE FORMS ARE A WAY OF STORING VITAL INFORMATION One of the biggest criticisms of review meetings is the form-filling part of the process; for most managers and staff it is a headache. The forms are not the purpose of the meeting; the forms should be a simple mechanism to record data and what was agreed during the meeting. They were designed to standardise the process and ensure fairness and objectivity.

Every company with a performance process in place will have some standardised forms available for their managers, along with guidelines to help complete them. Some will be handwritten forms; other companies are moving online. Whatever type of forms you have, ensure that you discuss the performance and goals before committing them to paper.

You should revamp your forms every three years to account for the evolving culture within your company. Keep looking for ways to make them more relevant to your day-to-day working environment. Consider changing the name from 'appraisal form' or 'review form' to 'Personal Business Plan'. This will highlight the link between individual and business goals.

Figure 4.12 provides a sample Personal Business Plan.

FIGURE 4.12 — SAMPLE OF A PERSONAL BUSINESS PLAN

<COMPANY LOGO>

PERSONAL BUSINESS PLAN <YEAR>

EMPLOYEE'S NAME	DEPARTMENT	MANAGER'S NAME

REVIEW OF SMARTER GOALS <PERIOD>

Summary of Organisational Business Goals for <year>

REVIEW OF SMARTER GOALS <PERIOD>

SUCCESS INDICATORS	SMARTER GOAL	BEST FEEDBACK	ASSESSMENT %
			EXCEEDED EXPECTATIONS ☐ MET EXPECTATIONS ☐ DID NOT MEET EXPECTATIONS ☐
			EXCEEDED EXPECTATIONS ☐ MET EXPECTATIONS ☐ DID NOT MEET EXPECTATIONS ☐
			EXCEEDED EXPECTATIONS ☐ MET EXPECTATIONS ☐ DID NOT MEET EXPECTATIONS ☐
			EXCEEDED EXPECTATIONS ☐ MET EXPECTATIONS ☐ DID NOT MEET EXPECTATIONS ☐
			EXCEEDED EXPECTATIONS ☐ MET EXPECTATIONS ☐ DID NOT MEET EXPECTATIONS ☐

FIGURE 4.12 CONT. — SAMPLE OF A PERSONAL BUSINESS PLAN

Overall Feedback on Personal Business Plan <year>

EMPLOYEE COMMENTS:

Overall Feedback on Personal Business Plan <year>

MANAGER COMMENTS:

SUMMARY OF SCORING TO USE:

120%	EXCEPTIONAL PERFORMANCE – 120% OF TARGET
110%	EXCEEDS EXPECTATIONS – 110% OF TARGET
100%	MEETS EXPECTATIONS – 100% OF TARGET
90%	DOES NOT MEET EXPECTATIONS – 90% OF TARGET
80%	DOES NOT MEET MINIMUM STANDARDS – 80% OF TARGET

SMARTER GOALS FOR <PERIOD>

KEY COMPANY GOALS <YEAR>

KEY TEAMS GOALS <YEAR>

INDIVIDUAL SMARTER GOALS <PERIOD>

Key Success Indicators	SMARTER Goals	Key actions to take

PERSONAL LEARNING AND DEVELOPMENT PLANS <PERIOD>

Learning & development needs identified	Alignment to business plan

<ADDITIONAL TOPICS AGREED ON AGENDA>

Further Comments	
SIGNED (EMPLOYEE):	DATE:
SIGNED (MANAGER):	DATE:

Closing the review meeting

Finish the meeting with your good performers on a positive note. Thank the person for their efforts and summarise their achievements during the review period. Discuss the next steps, including when you will have the documentation back to them. It's also important to schedule their next review meeting.

Quarterly review meetings as part of your performance culture

I would recommend that you hold quarterly review meetings at a minimum. Moving to quarterly reviews will support your high-performance culture and increase your chances of meeting all your business targets. One of the biggest misconceptions about quarterly reviews is that they take up too much time; this is due to many people's perceptions of annual reviews. However, both staff and managers find reviews conducted regularly are more engaging and beneficial to all parties because it is easier to discuss personal business plans, they are more relevant and current and they provide more opportunities to be involved with developing the business strategy.

Business decisions will be taken throughout the year that will affect your team's goals. During these quarterly meetings, you can officially update and realign everyone's individual goals while also signing off on previous goals. These meetings should last approximately 30 minutes. There are some helpful templates for these meetings in **Chapter 6**.

A presentation-style approach to review meetings

Once your team is comfortable preparing for and participating in their review meetings, you may need to freshen up your approach. Move away from the interview-style format and towards a presentation-style approach. By using this approach, your staff can deliver their business plan in a way that will open up real conversations about their performance and business strategy. The format encourages thorough preparation by everyone, gives you, the manager, an insight into whether everyone understands your key priorities and it also supports accountability.

Introducing a presentation style is straightforward and builds on the work you have already done. The main change is the style of delivery during the review meeting. Instead of sitting down around a round table inviting comments around SMARTER goals, the person will give a presentation telling their story.

In a presentation-style meeting, the agenda is the same but the delivery is different. The person being reviewed will open the meeting by explaining how they have performed against their targets. Similar to the traditional meeting, they will highlight their key goals and support their story with evidence. Then you will give your feedback and sign off on their performance.

The next stage of the presentation will cover the SMARTER goals for the next period, using the same structure as before. They will go on to discuss their personal learning and development plans and any other topic that was on the agenda. The key difference with this approach is that the person being reviewed takes responsibility for the content of the meeting. It also ensures that they are fully prepared for the meeting and that there is more involvement and ownership.

While this approach may not suit everyone, you should use it for your managers, sales team or people looking for promotion. It is a very engaging style of review and it will appeal to high performers.

AT A GLANCE — CHAPTER FOUR

You should spend approximately 30% of your allotted time discussing the period under review and 70% of the time outlining the goals and expectation levels for the next period. Review meetings should be future-based, using past performance to influence future performance.

The format and content of each meeting will vary, but using some thought-provoking questions will help to initiate a flowing, two-way conversation.

A productive meeting is conducted in five phases: introduction, review of previous period, SMARTER goal setting, career planning and documentation.

As a leader, you set the tone for the conversation. It is worth remembering that if you don't bring energy to the meeting, if you're not excited and enthusiastic about next year's plans or you don't engage your team in meaningful ways, then you shouldn't expect great things from your team.

The BEST feedback framework will help move from a blame culture to a responsibility culture in which people are energised and enthusiastic about improving their performance.

Setting key priorities using the SMARTER Way goal-setting system ensures that each goal has clarity, is challenging, promotes engagement and feeds into the business plan.

Expecting your team to grow and develop without your support is unrealistic. Your top talent need their careers to be managed effectively so that they will remain engaged and fulfil their potential.

The presentation-style approach encourages your staff to deliver their personal business plan in a way that will open up real conversations about their performance and business strategy.

CHAPTER FIVE

MANAGE THE TALENT, MANAGE CAREERS

5

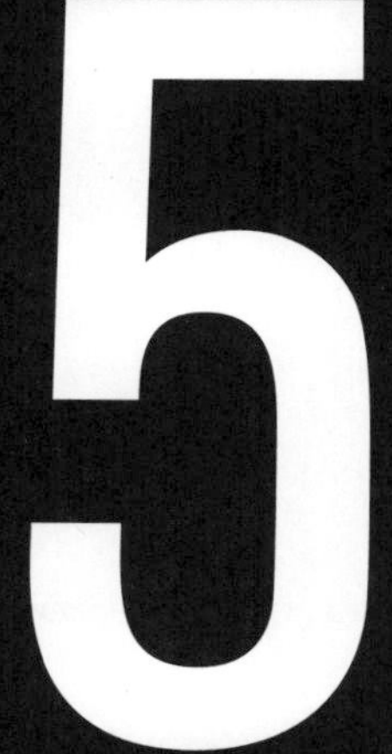

Manager: Alex, what training course will I put on your appraisal form for next year? I see last year you wanted some Excel training. Did you get any? I thought you were a wiz on those spreadsheets!

Alex: Well as it turned out, I wasn't allowed to go on a course because there was no budget for it last year, which was a pity. I really need an advanced course – it will save me a lot of time if I could learn how to write some more formulas.

Manager: OK, will I put you down for some Excel training then?

Alex: But what about the budget?

Manager: We'll see, but I need to write something in the 'Training Needs' box.

Alex: OK, but it's a waste of time.

Master of your career

In my book, *Slave to a Job, Master of your Career*, I outline how people can take control of their career instead of drifting along. I believe that people should manage their career in the same way that they would manage a business. Everyone has to take responsibility for their career and invest quality time in planning their development. This investment will help safeguard their future.

Everyone on your team has a career, but not everyone wants the same things from their career. As a leader, you need to ensure that you maximise the talent within your team, so it is important that you figure out what is important to each member of your team in terms of their careers. This will build great engagement and will support your efforts in building a high-performance culture.

By applying the PEAK Leadership principles you can align your team's career development with high performance. Figure 5.3 provides a recap on the PEAK Leadership core principles. Managing talent is important for maintaining high performance and ensuring that your succession plan is workable. A key way to do this is by introducing a personal learning and development plan for everyone on your team. This should be a practical and living document.

Benefits of personal learning and development plans

As a manager and leader, you must create a learning environment. "People cannot be ordered to manage their own learning" (Reid and Barrington, 1999) – they sometimes need guidance and support to identify their training requirements. Sustained personal development also requires a commitment from you, their manager, that learning is really valued. Encouraging people to fulfil their potential will impact positively on their performance.

FIGURE 5.1 — BENEFITS OF PLD PLANS FOR MANAGERS

- STRENGTHENS THE TALENT WITHIN YOUR TEAM.
- BUILDS A FLEXIBLE AND ADAPTABLE TEAM.
- IMPROVES PRODUCTIVITY LEVELS.
- ENSURES PEOPLE ARE COMPLIANT WITH REGULATIONS AND COMPANY POLICIES.
- DEVELOPS FUTURE LEADERS.
- IMPROVES THE ABILITY TO RESPOND TO CHANGE.

FIGURE 5.2 — BENEFITS OF PLD PLANS FOR STAFF

- ENHANCES PORTFOLIO OF SKILLS, KNOWLEDGE AND EXPERTISE.
- ADDS A SENSE OF DIRECTION AND PURPOSE TO CAREER DEVELOPMENT.
- HELPS TO EXCEED EXPECTATIONS.
- PROVIDES NECESSARY SKILLS FOR TODAY AND THE FUTURE.
- PROVIDES FLEXIBILITY WITHIN THE ORGANISATION.
- SHOWS THEY ARE VALUED.
- SHOWS MANAGEMENT IS INVESTED IN THEIR CAREERS.
- HELPS TO GAIN MARKETABLE SKILLS.

FIGURE 5.3 — PEAK LEADERSHIP PRINCIPLES

PERFORMANCE IS CHALLENGED

dentify the skills, knowledge and expertise that are required for your team. Constantly ask ourself: How can we improve? Why do we do it this way? What will our customers needs be in wo years? Is there a better or more efficient way?

E

ENVIRONMENT IS CREATED

upport your team's learning and development needs by creating a learning culture in vhich everyone helps to cross-train the team and learning and teaching is part of their goals or the year. Build an environment where it is safe to continually ask questions and push the oundaries of learning. Promote innovation and creativity.

ALIGN THE GOALS

lign all of your learning and development goals to your succession plan to ensure a sustainable igh-performing culture within your team. Know who your successor is and what they need to lo to gain the required experience. Align these goals to the company's business strategy.

KEEP STAFF ENGAGED

ink the team's career paths to their learning and development goals for the year. Ensure that they continuously update their personal learning and development plans to reflect their career progression. Explain how you can support their career ambitions, both in the short and long term.

PLD Plans – Five-step approach

Each personal learning and development (PLD) plan should clearly outline the individual's training programme, including its timeframe. The PLD plan details learning needs based on a thorough analysis, a log of training already completed and a route map for the next period. Although each PLD plan is a two-way commitment between the manager and team member, there is an emphasis on personal responsibility.

The five main steps in devising a PDL plan for each team member are shown in Figure 5.4.

FIGURE 5.4 — A FIVE-STEP APPROACH FOR BUILDING A PLD PLAN

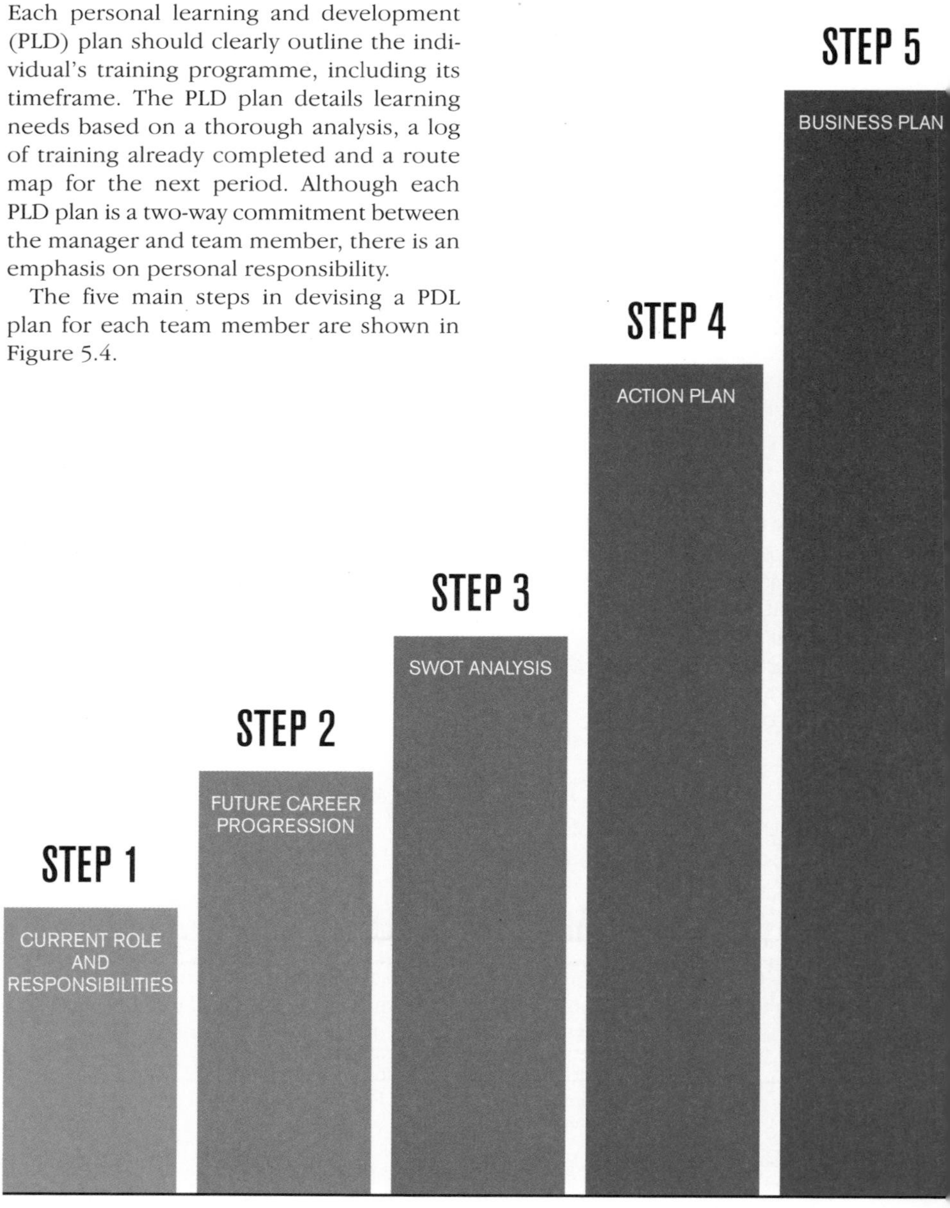

STEP 5

BUSINESS PLAN

STEP 4

ACTION PLAN

STEP 3

SWOT ANALYSIS

STEP 2

FUTURE CAREER PROGRESSION

STEP 1

CURRENT ROLE AND RESPONSIBILITIES

Step 1 – Current role and responsibilities

Begin the process by reviewing each person's current position. Build their profile by adding an addition column to the performance summary for their role (see **Chapter 3**). In this column list all key skills, knowledge and experience that are required for each indicator. This exercise also helps to align their PLD plans to tangible business results. Then identify any gaps that could affect performance levels.

FIGURE 5.5 — PERFORMANCE SUMMARY FOR EACH ROLE

PERFORMANCE INDICATOR	NECESSARY SKILLS, KNOWLEDGE AND EXPERIENCE
Business Goal Reduce by 5% the costs of running the business by the end of the first quarter.	The skills, knowledge and experience required for this goal include: • Influencing • Negotiation • Collaboration • Analysing • Communication • Understanding stationery requirements • Research • Report writing
Success Indicators for Alex She has taken on the role of looking after the stationery within the department. Has reviewed how much is spent on stationery by our department and identified areas of spending that could be cut without impacting negatively on the department. Has collaborated successfully with all stakeholders and has introduced a new ordering process that ensures we have enough stationery at all times while driving down costs through avoidable wastage. Has negotiated new terms with a supplier that can maintain the quality required and also within budget. Has successfully reduced costs by 28% by the end of Q1.	
SMARTER Goal Reduced the cost of stationery within the finance department by 28% by the end of Q1.	
Core Competency Use of influencing, negotiation and collaboration skills.	

Once you have collected all the data, you need to prioritise the learning and development requirements. This can be done by using the priority grid below.

The priority grid ensures that the PDL plans focus on the high-value activities. There is a tendency for some people to learn what they like rather than what they need. Each plan should follow the sequence of P1, P2 and then P3 (there is no reason to include any P4 activities).

FIGURE 5.6 — PRIORITY GRID

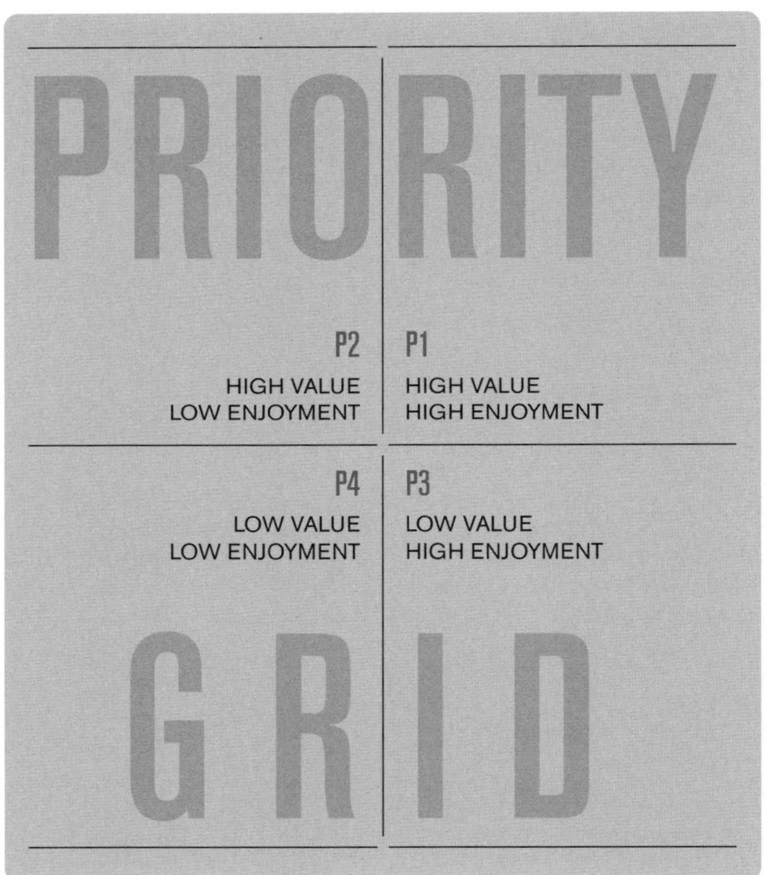

Step 2 – Future career/role progression
Once you have established the learning and development needs for today, you then need to look to the future. All great leaders have one eye on today and the other eye on tomorrow. Again, keep the conversation focused on the person's requirements. Discuss their career plans, where they see themselves in the future and where opportunities might be found.

Use open questions to keep the conversation flowing, examples of which are given in Figure 5.7.

FIGURE 5.7 — QUESTIONS TO EXPLORE CAREER AMBITIONS

What are you passionate about?

How can we support your career progression?

What type of work would you like to be doing in three years' time?

Where do you see the opportunities to further your career?

What skills do you need to develop that will give your career an advantage?

This part of the conversation is about their suitability for a future role or promotion. For example, someone on your team who is currently a semi-senior accountant has indicated that they would like to become a senior accountant by the end of the year. Gather all the data relevant to the senior role and discuss the key skills and experience required to fulfil this position. Identify the current skills gaps and then prioritise them. Include this as a separate part of their PLD plan.

For members of the team who are happy to remain in their current position you should discuss how you envisage their role developing over the next two to three years. Explain how their tasks might change and as a result what skills and experience they will need to update. So instead of discussing career progression, you focus the conversation on their role development.

FIGURE 5.8 — A PERFORMANCE INDICATOR FOR A POTENTIAL ROLE

POTENTIAL ROLE – SENIOR ACCOUNTANT

Performance Indicator	Necessary skills, knowledge and experience
SUCCESS INDICATORS:	
CORE COMPETENCIES:	

Step 3 – SWOT analysis

The third step is to carry out a SWOT (strengths, weaknesses, opportunities and threats) analysis. This is a comprehensive overview of the person's capabilities. The purpose of this part of the conversation is to help the person think about their development in broader terms.

The SWOT analysis will help you identify both the internal and external factors that will either help or prevent people achieving their career goals. It should also provide you with a list of actions they need to add to their PLD plans.

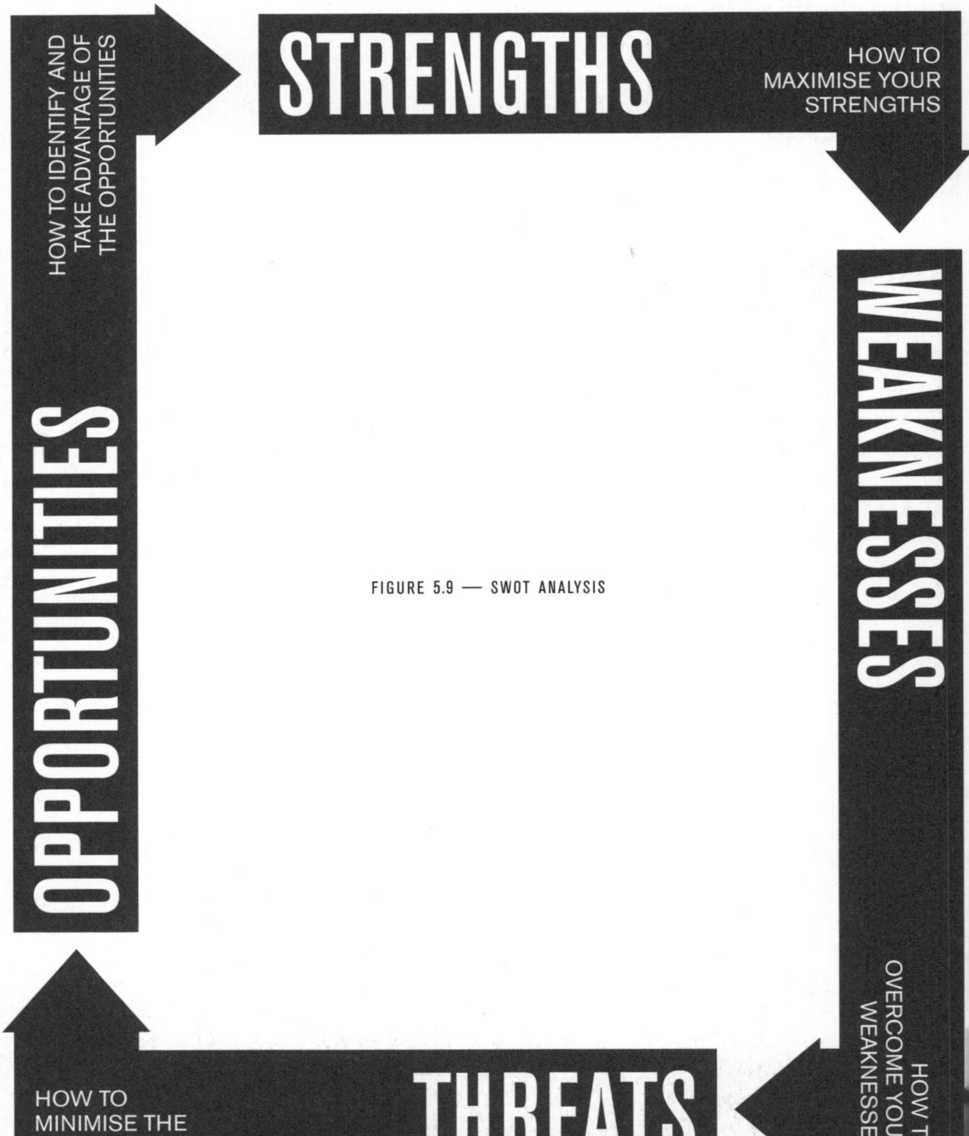

FIGURE 5.9 — SWOT ANALYSIS

STRENGTHS A person's list of strengths is the areas where they are performing strongly, and can be used as a competitive edge in career progression. In most cases their strengths were the reason you hired them in the first place. Review them quarterly to ensure that the person continuously develops their strengths and does not become complacent. Look on their strengths as assets that the PLD plans help to safeguard.

People generally work best when they are using the skills they like and have developed over the years, so consider whether you are fully utilising your team's full range of skills and knowledge. Figure 5.10 lists some questions you can ask to identify key strengths.

FIGURE 5.10 — QUESTIONS TO IDENTIFY STRENGTHS

What do you excel at in your current role?

What differentiates you from your colleagues or potential competitors?

Why do your customers/employers want you to keep working for them?

What are the main attributes of your 'personal brand'?

What are your top three skills?

What have you done to develop your strengths in the last six months?

What would we lose in terms of experience if you left?

WEAKNESSES The discussion around each team member's weaknesses should not be avoided or viewed as negative. This is a time when honest BEST feedback is required. When you identify the problem areas, you can start to build a picture of exactly where you are vulnerable. Seek out evidence that these weaknesses are real rather than perceived, for example someone may feel that their presentation skills are very poor when this may not be the case. Instead of sending them on a presentation training course, give them some positive feedback and exposure to more opportunities to present.

Once these weaknesses have been established, discuss with the person concerned how the weaknesses can be addressed before they become problems. You may not be able to eliminate the weaknesses completely, but you must reduce their impact on performance as much as possible. Figure 5.11 lists some questions you can ask to identify key weaknesses.

FIGURE 5.11 — QUESTIONS TO IDENTIFY WEAKNESSES

Do you have the skills required to exceed your customer/employer needs?

What does your customer/employer see as a weakness in you?

Do others outperform you?

Can you manage your current workload?

Can you take constructive feedback and use it to improve?

Are you good at prioritising your workload?

Do you understand your manager's key priorities?

What do your colleagues offer that you don't?

OPPORTUNITIES It is equally important to identify opportunities available for your team to develop their skills and gain more experience. Talented people are always looking to challenge themselves to be better and they seek out opportunities to take on additional interesting work or projects. This part of your analysis will aid your retention policy, as it will show your top people that you are actively looking at ways to support their careers. Some of these opportunities will be external to the team and may require a temporary secondment to another department to build their experience in other parts of the business. There are also lots of opportunities for further education and professional qualifications that may benefit some of your team. Figure 5.12 lists some questions you can ask to identify possible opportunities to learn and develop.

FIGURE 5.12 — QUESTIONS TO IDENTIFY OPPORTUNITIES

What future opportunities are available for you in the jobs market and what skills will you require to secure these roles?

Where are the secondment opportunities that will develop your skills and experience?

What work projects can you join?

In what other department could you use your skills, knowledge and expertise?

How are your skills transferable?

What key tasks can your manager delegate to you?

Who would be a good mentor for you?

What part of the business is growing and expanding?

IT HAPPENS One way to build experience is through secondment to another department or part of the business. It has been common in global companies for employees to move abroad and gain experience in other parts of the world. More recently, however, people are upskilling by being seconded to a major client to help with a short-term project. This is very beneficial in building strong relationships with your key clients as well as gaining insight into how they operate and what their real needs are. It's a great way to add real value for your client.

THREATS Small weaknesses can become major threats if they are left unchecked. Part of any good PDL plan is to look to the future and identify potential problems. For example, if market conditions changed in a year, would some of your team be using obsolete skills? A key quality of anyone with serious career ambitions is the ability to keep an eye on the long-term goal and take early action to avoid potential problems. Warren Buffett calls this *"adaptive intelligence"*.

Figure 5.13 lists some questions you can ask to identify potential threats.

FIGURE 5.13 — QUESTIONS TO IDENTIFY THREATS

What changes do you envisage in the business over the next three to five years that will negatively impact your career?

How could the skills and knowledge that you currently have become obsolete?

How much time have you invested in your learning and development needs that meet your industry's medium- and long-term requirements?

How transferable are your skills and experience?

What essential skills are missing from your skills bank for future job opportunities?

Have you ignored any warning signs that your performance might be levelling out or beginning to reduce?

What areas of your work do you struggle with?

SWOT ANALYSIS IN ACTION Conduct a separate, concise analysis for each member of your team. Once you have the four lists completed, prioritise the results based on the factors that impact the person's performance the most. Use the findings to identify the skills that require improvement and what action is required, and add it to the PLD plan. For example, if a weakness was "presentation skills in meetings with key clients", the actions could be presentation skills training and/or joining a local business group that practices public speaking skills.

FIGURE 5.14 — A SAMPLE SWOT ANALYSIS

NAME	DATE	DEPARTMENT	PERIOD

INTERNAL FACTORS

Strengths	Weaknesses
Strong overall performance during the year. Proactivity: took on two projects during the last quarter. Good at developing trainees.	Reluctant to manage upwards. Business development and networking. Presentation skills in meetings with key clients.

EXTERNAL FACTORS

Opportunities	Threats
Secondment to accounts payable. Additional qualification: Tax. Job sharing between Alex and Rachel.	Slowdown in the market. New technology available. Twice overlooked for a promotion.

You can also use the results to cross-develop the team. For example, if someone is particularly strong in one area, then they can coach someone who is weak in it. Review your list in a broader way by asking the following questions:

- How can we use our strengths to build the team?
- How can we use our strengths to minimise threats to the team?
- How can we avail of opportunities to keep everyone engaged?

Step 4 – Action plan

Once you have gathered all the data, you can start filling in the PLD plan. Careful consideration should be given to the particular types of events that would best suit the learning requirements. For example, some events will be external training workshops while others could be coaching sessions by the manager. The learning needs are broken down into three key components:

1. Success indicators and SMARTER goals for current role.
2. Potential personal development within the role and the team in general.
3. Overall career development within the company.

The key skills and experience in each area that requires development are listed first in the PLD plan. The second part of the form outlines what training events will support the learning. The form is then signed off by all stakeholders.

FIGURE 5.15 — PLD PLAN TEMPLATE

NAME	DEPARTMENT	MANAGER	LAST UPDATE

ANALYSIS

Success Indicators and SMARTER goals Reduce the cost of print stationery within each department by 28% across the organisation by the end of Q1	Key skills, knowledge & competencies for development Influencing skills and how to deal with difficult people
Potential future role within the team Looking after the training programme for new recruits	Key skills, knowledge & competencies for development Coaching skills and understanding how people learn
Career Progression Potential to be assistant manager within two years	Key skills, knowledge & competencies for development Managing people and how to delegate

STRATEGY

Learning event External training workshop – Influencing Work Colleagues	**When** 5 March	**Expected Outcome** Ability to deal with different types of people, overcome conflict situations and achieve target through collaboration with other departments
Learning event	**When**	**Expected Outcome**
Learning event	**When**	**Expected Outcome**
STAFF MEMBER'S SIGNATURE DATE	MANAGER'S SIGNATURE DATE	HR's SIGNATURE DATE

Step 5 – Business plan

The final step is to align everyone's PLD plans with the company's overall business strategy. List the key business objectives and check that each PLD plan will contribute to these objectives. It is easier to obtain a training budget if you can show how the required training will improve the business's results.

FIGURE 5.15 — PLD AND BUSINESS PLAN TEMPLATE

NAME	DEPARTMENT	MANAGER	LAST UPDATE

ANALYSIS

Business Plan	Individual	Development Needs
To reduce overall costs in the business by 5%	Success Indicators and SMARTER goal Reduce the cost of print stationery within each department by 28% across the organisation by the end of Q1	Key skills, knowledge & competencies for development Influencing skills and how to deal with difficult people
To become the employer of choice so that we will attract and retain the best employees	Potential future role within the team Looking after the training programme for new recruits	Key skills, knowledge & competencies for development Coaching skills and understanding how people learn
To build a leadership pipeline and retain the company's best talent	Career Progression Potential to be assistant manager within two years	Key skills, knowledge & competencies for development Managing people and how to delegate

STRATEGY

Learning event External training workshop – Influencing Work Colleagues	**When** 5 March	**Expected Outcome** Ability to deal with different types of people, overcome conflict situations and achieve target through collaboration with other departments
Learning event	**When**	**Expected Outcome**
Learning event	**When**	**Expected Outcome**
STAFF MEMBER'S SIGNATURE DATE	MANAGER'S SIGNATURE DATE	HR's SIGNATURE DATE

Self-analysis checklist

A self-analysis checklist (see Figure 5.16) is a great way to ensure that your team takes personal responsibility for moving their careers forward as planned. It gives people an at-a-glance view of the amount of effort that is required to maintain a great career, and it promotes accountability as evidence must be provided.

I recommend that your team completes this checklist on a monthly basis. Conducted monthly, these checklists provide you with a quick measure of the morale within the team, attitudes towards high performance and whether there are any performance blocks. By probing a little deeper, you may uncover some obstacles that you can remove quickly and easily.

You can tailor this checklist to meet the needs of your team. Discuss the outcomes at your monthly one-to-one meetings and start to build a learning and development culture that is focused on achieving outstanding results.

Delegation as a form of development

Effective delegation is part of your talent management strategy as it gives you an opportunity to evaluate your team while giving them an opportunity to demonstrate their abilities at a higher level. Too many managers see delegation as a way of offloading their work rather than as a way to evaluate and develop people. Consider using delegation as part of your coaching strategy.

When delegating a task to someone for the first time, avoid using vague instructions and making assumptions about their level of knowledge. Phrases like "there's no rush to get it to me; whenever you get a chance" or "use your initiative" aren't helpful and will create problems because people will interpret them differently.

Delegation that will develop people requires a six-step approach as described in Figure 5.17.

FIGURE 5.16 — A MONTHLY SELF-ANALYSIS CHECKLIST

MONTHLY REVIEW 12 WAYS TO SHOW THAT I EXCELLED THIS MONTH. "HAVE I PERFORMED TO MY POTENTIAL?"	
What evidence do I have to show that I achieved all of my goals set at the start of the month?	
What key goal did I achieve this month that set me apart?	
What obstacles did I overcome that highlight my core competencies?	
Have I delivered the best-quality service possible (show evidence)? If not, how could I have improved any part of my service?	
How have my time-management skills helped me improve my overall performance?	
Have I worked on my personal learning and development plan? If so, how has it improved my performance?	
How have I used my networking skills to add value to my career?	
Have I allowed the fear of criticism or failure to influence my performance? If so, to what extent?	
Have I worked effectively with all of my colleagues? If not, why and what will I do to overcome this problem?	
Have I allowed my energy levels to drop due to lack of motivation? If so, how will I re-energise myself?	
What did I do outside of work that improved my career prospects?	
What significant contribution did I make to my team this month?	

FIGURE 5.17 — A SIX-STEP APPROACH TO EFFECTIVE DELEGATION

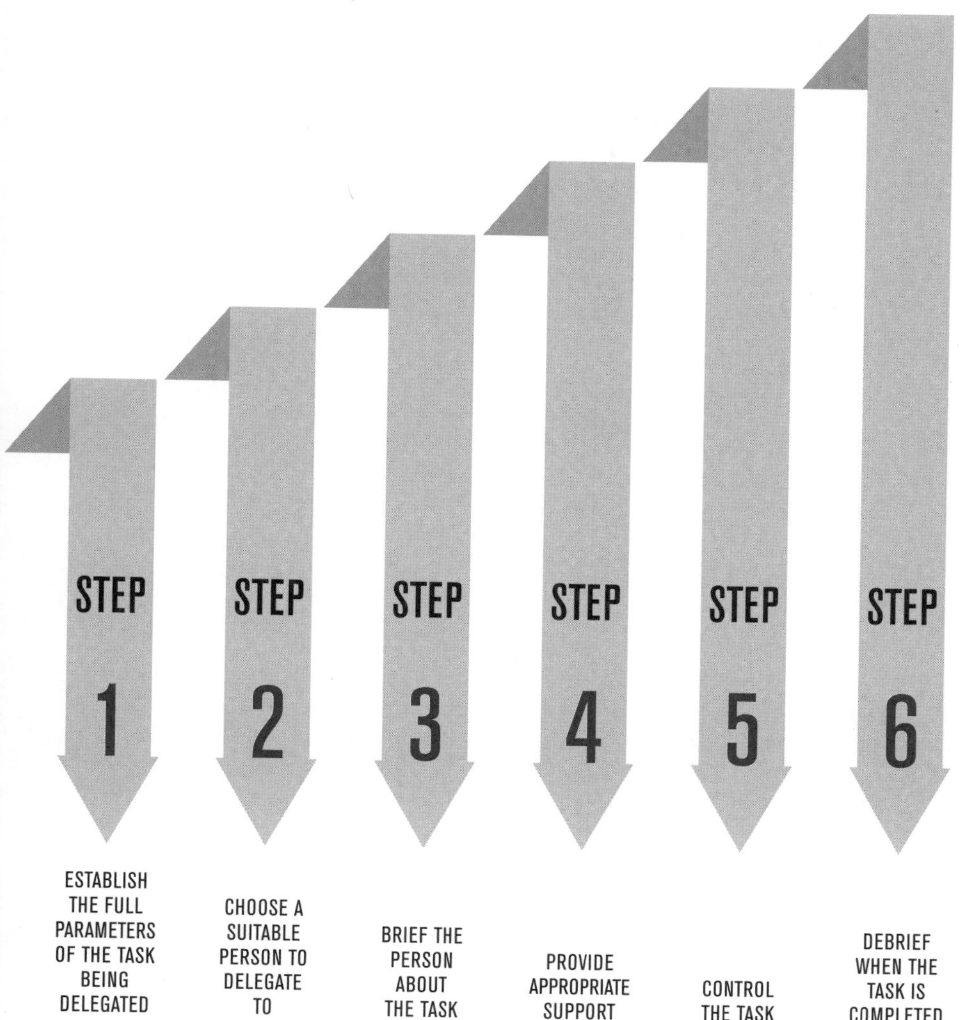
STEP 1
STEP 2
STEP 3
STEP 4
STEP 5
STEP 6
ESTABLISH THE FULL PARAMETERS OF THE TASK BEING DELEGATED
CHOOSE A SUITABLE PERSON TO DELEGATE TO
BRIEF THE PERSON ABOUT THE TASK
PROVIDE APPROPRIATE SUPPORT
CONTROL THE TASK
DEBRIEF WHEN THE TASK IS COMPLETED

Step 1 – Establish the full parameters of the task

Think about all of the requirements of the task (success indicators) you are proposing to delegate. You need to have a full understanding of what you want completed as well as how you want the job done. You must be able to convey this information in a way that will be clearly understood by the person who will complete the task. Outline their responsibilities, the standard expected and give clear timelines. Finally, determine the tasks priority level so that there is no misunderstanding around its importance relevant to the other work on the person's desk. Create a summary note to eliminate any assumptions or misconceptions about your requirements.

FIGURE 5.18 — SUMMARY OF STEP 1

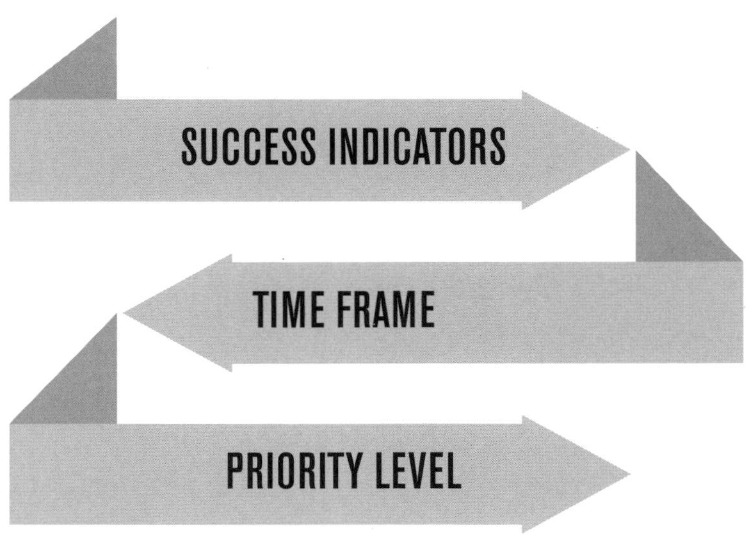

Step 2 – Choose a suitable person

Choosing a suitable person involves more than merely naming someone to do the task. For delegation to work, you need to consider the person's attitude, capabilities and skill levels. Then you need to weigh up your options and determine what level of support they will require. Always improve motivation (attitude) first and then work on improving their skill levels. Ideally, you should also figure out how the delegated task will enhance their career progression. Remember, you are using delegation as a tool to manage and coach your top talent.

Also consider their current workload to establish if they have sufficient time to learn a new task and deliver it to the expected level. You may need to reassign some tasks or reprioritise their workload.

Step 3 – Brief the person about the task

Take your time when explaining the delegated task. Investing time at this stage will reduce errors and misunderstandings. Describe success indicators for the task and how it fits into the business plan. Explain why you have chosen them for this task and how they will benefit from the skills learned in completing the task to the expected standard.

If the person is doing the task for the first time, ask them to explain their understanding of what you want to achieve and how you want them to approach this task. This will help with clarity and also identify areas that may require additional support. Be on the lookout for any ambiguity or uncertainty. For a person who is doing the task for a second or third time, focus on the areas that they struggled with the last time.

Although the manager is ultimately still responsible for the quality of the task, effective delegation ensures that the person takes ownership and completes the task at the expected level.

IT HAPPENS "Rachel, I need a report on this case when you get the chance. I know you haven't done it before, but I'm sure you'll be fine. I'm heading out to a meeting but if you have any problems, Alex or Tom will help you when they get back. It that alright? See you later."

The biggest problem with delegation is making too many assumptions combined with a lack of clarity. Delegation on the run can be costly.

Step 4 – Provide appropriate support
It is important at this stage of the discussion to outline the support that you will provide, especially if the person lacks confidence or experience. If their skill level is low, you may offer some training before they start the task. For example, they could sit beside a colleague who is performing the task and learn how to do it. For a more complicated task, they may need to go on a formal training course.

Keep the lines of communication open and be available to answer their questions. Avoid giving the answers all the time, building trust instead by encouraging them to figure out the solutions – they may even find a better way of doing the job.

Step 5 – Control the task
All tasks, including delegated tasks, must be monitored and their progress evaluated so that the desired results are achieved. Always put your controls in place prior to commencing the task. This prevents people thinking that you are checking up on them if you prefer tight controls. If you like loose controls, it will prevent people believing that you have abandoned them. Agreeing benchmarks upfront will help everyone focus on the timelines and outcomes. It's also a good idea to control when they can ask questions by agreeing check-in times during the day. Ensure that people understand that they must report any problems to you as soon as they arise.

Step 6 – Debrief when the task is complete
This final stage is often overlooked in the haste to move on to the next piece of work. If it is ignored, however, vital information could be lost because you didn't invest five to 10 minutes reviewing how the person got on with the task. It is also a great opportunity to reflect on the experience the person gained and what was learned by all parties.

Figure 5.19 lists some examples of questions you could ask during a debrief session.

FIGURE 5.19 — DEBRIEFING QUESTIONS

What support would you need the next time you do the task?

What advice would you give the next person who will do this task?

What did you learn?

What was your biggest challenge?

What did you like most about this task?

FIGURE 5.19 CONT. — DEBRIEFING QUESTIONS

What did you like least about this task?

How did this task help with your career progression?

How clear were the instructions?

What do you now know (but didn't know before completing the task) that you could use in the future?

What would make it easier the next time?

Would you like to do this task again?

AT A GLANCE

CHAPTER FIVE

Everyone in your team has a career, but not everyone wants the same things from their career. By applying the PEAK Leadership principles you can align your team's career development with high performance.

Use a five-step approach so that each personal learning and development (PLD) plan will clearly outline the individual's training programme:

1. Review each person's current position.
2. Discuss their career plans, where they see themselves in the future, and where they see opportunities.
3. Conduct a SWOT analysis to look at both internal and external factors that affect your team's learning and development. You can conduct a separate analysis for each member of your team.
4. Analyse the results and fill in the PLD plan.
5. Align everyone's PLD plans with the company's overall business strategy.

Everyone on your team should have at least one learning and development goal for each quarter. This will ensure that learning and development takes place throughout the year.

A self-analysis checklist is a great way to ensure that your team takes personal responsibility for moving their careers forward as planned.

Use delegation to coach your team. Effective delegation is part of your talent management strategy as it gives you the opportunity to evaluate your team while giving them an opportunity to demonstrate their abilities at a higher level.

CHAPTER SIX

DEALING WITH POOR PERFORMANCE

Manager: Alex is just a lost cause. She is performing way below standard. You need to do something about her. Can you sack her?

HR Manager: That's a bit drastic, have you spoken to Alex about her performance? Have you pointed out how she can improve?

Manager: She knows I'm not happy; I took her off the payment project last month. Surely that's a sign that even she would recognise.

HR Manager: I'm just looking at her last review and you gave her a rating of 100% – meets all expectations. You even mentioned that she is a hardworking and important member of the team. My hands are tied here. You have to deal with Alex fairly and give her a chance to improve; speak to her about her performance.

Manager: How do I do that without creating friction in the team? Can't you have a word?

HR Manager: Managing the team is your responsibility. I'm here to give you as much support and guidance as you need, but you must deal with any performance issues.

Poor performance happens at some point

Work that is below the expected standard happens on occasion, even to your best people. In some situations it is a small blip in an otherwise excellent review; for others it becomes symptomatic of their overall performance.

Dealing with people who aren't performing can be very difficult and stressful for some managers, and there are many reasons why managers are reluctant to confront underperformance. For some there is a genuine concern that their corrective actions will make matters worse or that the individual may react badly to their feedback. In some cases managers simply don't like criticising anyone on their team because they need to be liked, or worry that it could create a negative working environment.

If you avoid the issue of poor performance, however, the problem will usually worsen and start to affect the entire team's performance. You will end up with a larger and often far more time-consuming and stressful problem to deal with. Research shows that someone who is underperforming rarely improves without some direct intervention.

Ignoring the problem isn't an option.

What is poor performance?

There are many factors that contribute to the quality of someone's work, including their skills, knowledge, attitude, aptitude, appearance and ability. This makes defining 'poor performance' a little more complicated. In some situations underperformance is more behavioural than results-oriented. For example, a person may achieve all of their business targets but their attitude and behaviour towards their colleagues isn't acceptable and has caused problems. This form of underperformance is often ignored because the person has met their business targets. However, it eventually leads to poor performance in others. It could also lead to talented people leaving your team as they become disillusioned and frustrated with their colleague's poor behaviour.

Before you can successfully address performance issues, you must define poor performance. Take a broader view on performance; define the behavioural aspects of the task as well as the functional parts. A clear understanding of this part of the job will make gathering evidence to support your view a lot easier. Always focus on the facts, particularly when you are discussing sensitive areas such as attitude, appearance or ability.

IT HAPPENS Manager: "Her work is excellent and she really knows her stuff. My only problem is that her general appearance isn't at the standard that we expect at our firm. I personally wouldn't be comfortable bringing her to meet clients as she dresses too casually. Also her personal hygiene can be lacking on occasions. I have sent an e-mail to everyone reminding them of our dress code, but that only worked for a week or so. I don't want to lose her, but what can I do?"

Sending general e-mails to the entire team in an attempt to deal with a performance issue, as is often the case for managers who are reluctant to take corrective action, isn't the solution. A planned approach is required.

Some general factors that cause performance issues

There are some common factors in poor performance, such as a lack of confidence, poor time management or lack of focus. It is always worth examining these areas to assess whether they play a part in the problem.

To prevent underperformance from happening in the first place, you should regularly review these factors by asking some simple questions; early identification and intervention will save you a lot of time and hassle. These factors and questions are detailed in Figure 6.1.

FIGURE 6.1 — FACTORS INFLUENCING THE PERFORMANCE OF PEOPLE ON YOUR TEAM

LACK OF SELF-CONFIDENCE 1

A lack of self-confidence is often the result of poor support or training from management. People are expected to understand their role from end to end and also be an expert on your full range of products/services. In addition, their job was never fully explained to them, which means people might be unsure of the importance of their role, how they fit into the company or the value of their day-to-day tasks.

- Do they know what is expected of them all the time?
- Were they fully trained to do their job?
- Do they understand the importance of their role?
- Do they get regular feedback on their performance?
- Are their opinions sought and listened to?

MOTIVATION 2

As professionals, your team have a responsibility to motivate themselves every day. This requires a lot of self-discipline and focus. Top sportspeople analyse each component of their performance so that they can make small but consistent improvements.

Similarly, an effective way to motivate people in work is to monitor their performance against their targets on a daily basis. Set SMARTER goals that challenge them and then track their progress in real time. The key to achieving key goals is to track progress.

- Do they contribute to writing the success indicators for the team?
- Do they set their own SMARTER goals?
- Do they benchmark their progress against their peers?
- Do they monitor their own performance?
- Are they fully engaged?

FIGURE 6.1 CONT. — FACTORS INFLUENCING THE PERFORMANCE OF PEOPLE ON YOUR TEAM

POOR TIME MANAGEMENT 3

Time management is one of the most important skills for your team. "Time management isn't about managing time, it's about managing yourself and those around you and let time take care of itself" (Sean McLoughney, 2008). It turns good workers into outstanding workers.

- Do they have enough time and are they spending it wisely?
- Do they know how to prioritise effectively?
- Do they schedule their tasks daily, monthly and yearly?
- Do they conduct a regular time audit?
- Do they allocate time frames to their tasks?

LAZINESS 4

Giving up after encountering the first obstacle is something many managers unknowingly encourage in their team. They create 'lazy' people by correcting their mistakes instead of coaching, answering the same questions three or four times and becoming a safety net. Too many managers choose the quick and immediate action rather than the more thoughtful option, which is teaching.

- Do you correct or teach when someone makes a mistake?
- Do you delegate effectively?
- Do you encourage a learning environment?
- Do you invest time in developing your team?
- Do you encourage people to work things out for themselves?

LACK OF FOCUS OR DIRECTION 5

A lack of focus on key priorities can cause poor performance even in a hardworking person. This usually happens when their efforts are directed towards the wrong areas. This can be very demoralising for someone who is working extremely hard but is told that they are underperforming.

- Do they know exactly how they are performing against target?
- Do they know what your key priorities are?
- Can they pinpoint the targets they are behind on and then concentrate their energy on improving?
- Do they understand how they can contribute to the business plan?
- Do you hold regular meetings to discuss key strategies?

COMFORT ZONE 6

Everyone has their own comfort zones, a way of working that feels relaxed and easy to do. Most people are drawn to routine tasks and they build predictability into daily activities. In an ever-changing work environment, however, this can lead to a poor performance.

- Do you promote job rotation in your team?
- Do you encourage job secondment?
- Do you seek out new projects for your team?
- Do you send people on external training courses?
- Do you actively encourage work process improvement?

LIMITED TIME 7

Most people work within limited time frames based mainly on traditional working hours. As a result your team must use their time wisely, which means availing of technology whenever possible. Encourage the automation of tasks that are both time-consuming and non-profit-making.

- Do they analyse how they spend their time and establish where their time is being wasted?
- Do they complete time audits?
- Do they regularly review their time balance sheet (time available vs. time required)?
- Do they work beyond their core times?
- Do they know how to say 'no'?

JOB KNOWLEDGE 8

You may have hired the best person for the job, but you still need to explain their role and how it impacts other people within the company. Every job is different, so take the time to equip your team with the right tools and knowledge to perform their duties as expected.

- Do they fully understand their role?
- Has their role changed in the last six months?
- Have they been fully trained in their role?
- How does their role impact other people?
- Do they rely on others to complete tasks?

SKILLS ANALYSIS 9

Complete a skills audit on your team to establish potential skills gaps. This data will help you formulate a coaching strategy and may prevent future poor performance.

- Does everyone on your team receive enough coaching?
- Where are your potential skills gaps for next year?
- Which skills are essential for high performance?
- Which skills will no longer be significant in the future?
- Do you carry out skills audits? If so, how often?

BENCHMARKING 10

Benchmark each person against the best people on your team and encourage people to learn from their colleagues. Reviewing your results in isolation doesn't give you the complete picture. Compare individual performances against their peers within the company. Use this data as a reference point for identifying areas for improvement. Don't reinvent the wheel; use benchmarking to improve performance. If appropriate, share this information with the team.

- Does your team actively benchmark themselves against each other?
- Do you encourage peer learning?
- Do you encourage your team to openly compare and discuss their performance with each other?
- Do you encourage self-analysis within your team?
- Do you benchmark the team against industry performance?

The consequences of avoiding the issues

Most managers avoid sitting down to have a difficult conversation with someone because it can be an uncomfortable experience for all. Emotions often run high and people can become angry and defensive. Unfortunately, avoidance merely prolongs the problem. Failure to act as soon as you notice someone is not performing can make the situation worse and have a direct impact on the business. Clients can become upset with the level of service that they are experiencing and start to look elsewhere, or the rest of the team may start to feel demoralised and disillusioned if they are forced to carry extra workloads. Worryingly, they may believe – because of your inaction – that mediocrity is acceptable and that this is the new standard. It is very unfair to your team to accept differing standard levels for individuals who do the same work and have the same capabilities. You must take decisive action and address all issues as soon as they arise.

Turning poor performance into great performance

While most managers have to address poor performance at some point in their career, many can be unsure of the best way to tackle the problem or prevent it from occurring in the first place. Most companies will issue guidelines to their managers (always refer to your company's procedure/HR guidelines before dealing with underperformance), but Figure 6.2 lists some general tips that can help.

Managing poor performance should focus on improvements rather than punishment. Ensure that all the steps you take treat the person fairly and with dignity. Putting a robust process in place will help you to implement a consistent approach to addressing performance issues.

There are five steps in turning poor performance around. Discuss performance issues in private; book a room or use your office and give the person some notice. During these meetings you should discuss and clarify expectations (both the what and how); give BEST feedback on the specific performance issue; agree a way forward with a structured performance improvement plan (PIP); outline how and when you will monitor their progress and, finally, at a later meeting, sign off on a completed PIP.

Earlier we saw how important it is to draft clear success indicators and SMARTER goals combined with a BEST feedback culture in order to drive a high-performing environment for your team. These frameworks can equally be used as the foundation for turning poor performance into the performance that you expect from everyone.

FIGURE 6.2 — A FIVE-STEP APPROACH TO ADDRESSING POOR PERFORMANCE

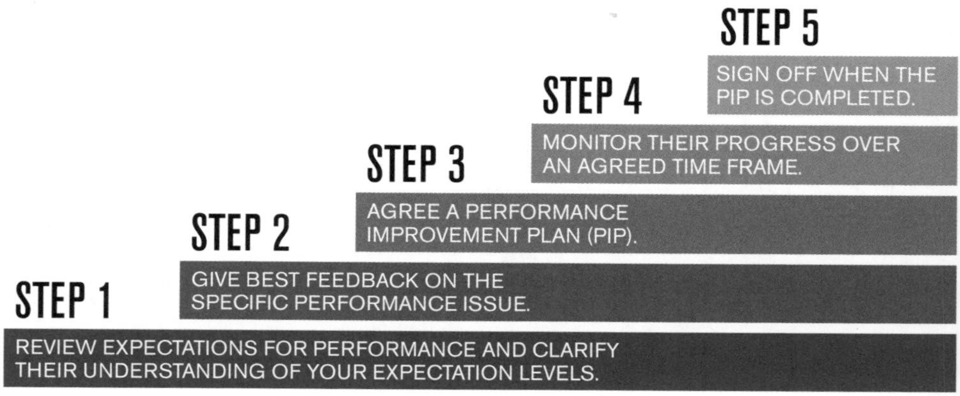

STEP 5
SIGN OFF WHEN THE PIP IS COMPLETED.

STEP 4
MONITOR THEIR PROGRESS OVER AN AGREED TIME FRAME.

STEP 3
AGREE A PERFORMANCE IMPROVEMENT PLAN (PIP).

STEP 2
GIVE BEST FEEDBACK ON THE SPECIFIC PERFORMANCE ISSUE.

STEP 1
REVIEW EXPECTATIONS FOR PERFORMANCE AND CLARIFY THEIR UNDERSTANDING OF YOUR EXPECTATION LEVELS.

Step 1 – Review expectations for performance
Set up a meeting as soon as you notice an issue with someone's performance. The purpose of this initial meeting is to improve performance; it is not a disciplinary issue at this stage. Therefore, the focus is on the actions that can be taken to move forward. It is important that the person is aware of the purpose of the meeting and that they are open and ready to participate.

The underlying causes of underperformance can vary greatly, so it is important that you establish the real issues before looking for a solution. Underperformance generally occurs when someone is unsure of what is expected of them, is lacking the ability or confidence to complete their tasks or is simply not motivated. A common mistake made by managers is assuming that all poor performance is motivational or ability related – more often it's inadequate communication of expectation levels.

The root cause of some underperformance issues can start as early as the goal-setting part of the review meeting. Start your analysis by examining the person's understanding of your expectations for the success indicator and the specific SMARTER goal at the centre of the issue. Ask them to explain the expected outcomes for this goal. Don't give any feedback on their performance at this stage. Next, ask them to outline how they think you expect them to achieve this goal. This will enable you to establish if there is a communication problem.

Step 2 – Feedback
Once you are satisfied that the person understands what is expected of them, you can then move to providing feedback. Honest and timely feedback is essential in creating a high-performance culture. It is also critical in turning poor performance around. However, according to Steve Foley, "you need to be brave with feedback". He reminds his managers at the start of every performance review period that they must view feedback as part of their role. Honest feedback requires bravery, as the person receiving it may not want to hear what you have to say.

Make feedback a part of everyday communication by regularly discussing performance, both good and bad. Outline where people are now and what they need to address in order to stay on track to achieving their goals. If you hold these discussions regularly, people will be comfortable talking to you about their performance and any issues that you might have with them.

If you have created such a 'feedback culture' within your team, this part of the conversation should be straightforward. Timely intervention keeps everyone focused on the expected performance level. Use the BEST feedback framework in the same way as you did in the review meeting (see Figure 6.4).

FIGURE 6.3 — INTRODUCING THE MEETING

1	2	3
EXPLAIN THE PURPOSE OF THE MEETING	OUTLINE THE AGENDA	SEEK CLARITY AROUND THE EXPECTATION OF THE SPECIFIC GOAL

FIGURE 6.4 — THE BEST FEEDBACK FRAMEWORK

B	E	S	T
BEHAVIOUR & IMPACT	**ESTABLISH CAUSE**	**SOLUTION / SUGGESTION**	**TIME**
Behaviour and impact: always discuss the person's behaviour and not their personality or attitude. Explain what they did, why it is not acceptable and what impact it had on their performance and the performance of the team.	Establish the root cause of the problem: was it lack of clarity, ability or motivation?	Solution: discuss the solution in detail, ensure the person takes personal responsibility for turning their performance around and is committed to improving.	Time frame: outline a time frame for improvement and any training requirements. Agree some benchmarks to monitor progress.

Begin your feedback by summarising the performance gap. This is the difference between the performance expected by you (and discussed in Step 1) and the performance delivered by the person. Base this assessment on facts and provide evidence to support your findings. Invite the person to comment on this gap. It is important at this stage that the person acknowledges that there is a gap before establishing the reasons for it.

Ask some probing questions to determine the real cause of the performance gap (see Figure 6.5). Prepare these questions in advance so that you can concentrate on listening to the answers. Listen very carefully to their explanation and establish whether or not the problem is within their control. For example, you might discover that the issue concerns workflows or resourcing levels. If it is outside their control, you must acknowledge this fact and take steps to rectify the situation.

However, the problem is usually within the person's control. At this stage of the conversation you need to focus on the cause: communication, skill or motivation? Keep asking the questions until you are totally satisfied that you identified the true reason.

Feedback should focus on the desired outcome. It is a mechanism to correct performance and keep people on track. The discussion should be beneficial to both people and be action-oriented.

FIGURE 6.5 — QUESTIONS TO ASK TO ESTABLISH THE ROOT CAUSE OF THE PROBLEM

Do they have the necessary skills and knowledge to complete their tasks to the expected standard?

Are the tasks clearly stated and understood by the person?

What training have they undertaken that will help them achieve their goals?

Do they have the necessary resources to complete their tasks?

Are there any personal or work-related issues that are affecting the person's performance?

Do they rely on others to complete their tasks?

Is the issue outside their control?

Step 3 – Agree a way forward

Real and lasting change in the way a poor performer behaves can only take place in an enabling and supportive environment. If the issue is small, then bringing it to the person's attention in an informal way is usually all that is necessary. Sit the person down and give them your BEST feedback, then agree a way forward and decide when your next meeting should take place. For example, if their knowledge and skills are low, offer support through training and coaching. Ask them if they need to sit with someone more experienced in order to up-skill. If their motivation is low, build your relationship with them so that you can identify their motivational triggers. Explain the value of their work and how it impacts the overall business plan. Whatever action you agree to take, it is best to keep a note on file for future reference. This note is an informal record for yourself and doesn't normally need to be passed on to HR. However, it is best practice to work within the guidelines of your company.

You should move to a more formal process (not your disciplinary process, if possible) if there is no improvement or if the under-performance escalates. A performance improvement plan (PIP) is a written contract between a manager and a direct report. (The involvement of HR at this stage varies from company to company. Check your staff handbook or HR for clarity.)

The PIP is a formal document that outlines what was discussed in the meeting and lists all the agreed actions. It also communicates clearly how and when progress will be measured. Its main purpose is to get people back to performing at the expected standard. It is not a method of punishment; it is a process built around support and clarity. It helps your underperformer to clearly understand what steps they need to take to improve their standard of work. The PIP should be linked into your quarterly or half-yearly reviews.

There is another practical reason to use a PIP. Sometimes people simply don't know how to improve their performance. They are stuck doing the same things in a belief that working harder will improve the situation. Their PIP and, more importantly, the discussion that took place in order to write it, will guide them back to performing as expected. A PIP should be seen as a positive step forward.

You can use a simple document (similar to Figure 6.6) to record all the relevant information for a performance improvement plan. Both parties should have a written copy of the PIP.

FIGURE 6.6 — A TEMPLATE PERFORMANCE IMPROVEMENT PLAN (PIP)

<COMPANY NAME AND LOGO>

PERFORMANCE IMPROVEMENT PLAN (PIP)

NAME	DEPARTMENT	TITLE
MANAGER	START DATE	END DATE

PERFORMANCE IMPROVEMENT PLAN (PIP) – ACTIONS

Performance improvement plans are part of our day-to-day management process and high-performance culture. This PIP is designed to clearly communicate the areas that you need to improve. It outlines what you need to do and how and when your progress will be measured. Its main purpose is to get you back to performing at the standard expected of you.

YOUR KEY AREAS OF FOCUS FOR IMPROVEMENT

<NAME>, while you have many strengths and capabilities that benefit <company name>, there are areas where improvement is necessary, and must be addressed immediately. Please read these carefully and discuss them with your manager.

Area(s) Requiring Improvement	Current Performance	Expectations – Success Indicators	Measurement – SMARTER goal	Training and Development needs
1.				
2.				
3.				

This is a serious process that must be completed within the agreed time frames. If the required improvements are not achieved, this may lead to disciplinary action up to and including dismissal. However, we are committed to supporting your efforts to meet the expected performance levels. We believe that, through a positive outlook coupled with hard work and commitment, the goals in this plan can definitely be achieved.

DECLARATION

I will work with my manager to meet the goals of this performance improvement plan.

EMPLOYEE SIGNATURE:	DATE:
MANAGER SIGNATURE:	DATE:
HR SIGNATURE:	DATE:

<EMPLOYEE NAME>

PIP SCHEDULE AND PROGRESS NOTES

WEEK 1
<DATE W/E>

Area to Improve – SMARTER Goal	Target for the week	Achieved	BEST Feedback
1.			
2.			
3.			

WEEK 2
<DATE W/E>

Area to Improve – SMARTER Goal	Target for the week	Achieved	BEST Feedback
1.			
2.			
3.			

Step 4 – Monitor the progress

The first part of the PIP is agreeing the actions to take, which is then written into the PIP document and signed and dated by all parties. The second part is to agree how and when progress will be monitored. It is important to give the person enough time to turn things around. This can vary from one to three months depending on their role and the complexity of the tasks in question.

Outline what their targets are on a weekly basis and what evidence of improvement they need to produce. This ensures that there are no ambiguities or misunderstandings. Meet to discuss this information weekly and record the proceedings. This is a formal record and can be referred to if the performance doesn't improve.

Step 5 – Sign off when the PIP is completed

At the end of the agreed time period for the PIP, there are three potential outcomes:

1. The performance hasn't improved.
2. The person decides to leave.
3. The performance now meets the required standard.

<DATE FROM> - <DATE TO>

WEEK 3
<DATE W/E>

Area to Improve – SMARTER Goal	Target for the week	Achieved	BEST Feedback
1.			
2.			
3.			

WEEK 4
<DATE W/E>

Area to Improve – SMARTER Goal	Target for the week	Achieved	BEST Feedback
1.			
2.			
3.			

Where the performance has not improved, you could choose to extend the PIP (particularly if there is a real sign of improvement or the person didn't have an opportunity to work on the task in question). The other option is to move the person onto the formal disciplinary process. Consult with your HR department for advice when dealing with any disciplinary action; ensure you follow the process according to the guidelines in your staff handbook.

The person may come to the conclusion that the role isn't suitable and decide to leave. Sometimes they will leave the company; however, in many situations they transfer to another department and become a valuable asset to their new team. The main purpose of the PIP is to retain good people because it is more cost effective. Moving someone to a more suitable role benefits all parties.

The most common outcome, however, is performance improvement. Once the performance has been turned around it is important to formally acknowledge this improvement. You need to sign off on the PIP so that the person under review is aware that the process has been successfully completed. Send them a letter (see Figure 6.7) to confirm this and keep a copy on their file.

FIGURE 6.7 — LETTER OF SUCCESSFUL COMPLETION OF PIP

PRIVATE & CONFIDENTIAL

<Date>

For the attention of: <Name>
<Department>

Re: Performance Improvement Plan – <Date that plan refers to>

Dear <Name>

After being placed on our formal performance improvement plan ("PIP") during the period <to>, I am pleased to confirm that you are now achieving the standard of performance that is required and expected from you in your current role. Therefore we do not see a need to extend the period any further.

I look forward to seeing your productivity and attitude towards your role (and colleagues and clients) continue at the standards that we have agreed and that you have demonstrated throughout the review period. I also need to advise you that, should there be a relapse where your performance and/or behaviour is brought into question again, you would be placed on a further review or even subject to disciplinary action.

Thank you for the effort and professionalism that you have shown in tackling the issues so positively.

Yours sincerely,

<Manager's name>
<Position>

FIGURE 6.8 — PEAK LEADERSHIP PRINCIPLES AND THE PIP

P

PERFORMANCE IS CHALLENGED

Use a PIP as a roadmap to demonstrate how your underperformer can improve their performance by taking specific actions.

E

ENVIRONMENT IS CREATED

Move from the negativity of discussing poor performance to a more positive conversation around the actions that the person can take to improve. Encourage them to take ownership and responsibility for the quality of their work and remain action-oriented. Use weekly updates to monitor progress.

ALIGN THE GOALS

Explain the impact that each action in their PIP has on the business in general and on their own personal goals.

KEEP STAFF ENGAGED

Show how successfully completing the PIP will impact the business plan. People are more engaged when they know that their efforts are worthwhile and make a difference. Highlight the value of their work and how it is part of something bigger. Acknowledge their progress and sign off when their PIP is completed.

(*PLEASE NOTE THAT THESE GUIDELINES ARE OF A GENERAL NATURE AND YOU SHOULD ALWAYS FOLLOW YOUR COMPANY'S GUIDELINES AND POLICIES, AS WELL AS CONTRACTUAL OBLIGATIONS.)

Review meetings and PIPs

The PIP meeting should never take place during your annual or quarterly review meetings – they need to be held as soon as performance becomes an issue. However, it is good practice to acknowledge the PIP during the review meetings, commenting on successful completions and the efforts that were put into it. You can also remind people of the expected standards and the consequences for poor performance.

Improving poor performance

Improving poor performance is part of your day-to-day managerial role and the PIP is an integral tool for doing that. By applying the PEAK Leadership, principles you can also align the PIP with your high-performing culture. The use of PEAK Leadership in the context of the PIP is outlined in Figure 6.8.

AT A GLANCE CHAPTER SIX

Work that is below the expected standard happens on occasions, even to your best people. In some situations it is a small blip in an otherwise excellent review; for others it becomes symptomatic of their overall performance.

Before you can successfully address performance issues, you must define 'poor performance'. Take a broader view of what constitutes poor performance: define the behavioural aspect of the task as well as the functional part.

There are five steps to turning poor performance around: discuss and clarify expectations (both the what and how); give BEST feedback on the specific performance issue; agree a way forward with a structured performance improvement plan (PIP); outline how and when you will monitor their progress; and finally, at a later meeting sign off on a completed PIP.

It is good practice to acknowledge the PIP during review meetings, commenting on successful completion and the efforts that were put into it. You can also remind people of the expected standards and the consequences for poor performance.

CHAPTER SEVEN
FOLLOW THROUGH

IT HAPPENS Manager: That's your appraisal finished for this year, Alex. At least we won't have to go through all that again until next year. All this form-filling drives me insane. Only another three to do.

Alex: Do you need me to follow up on anything?

Manager: No, I'll write up the forms and you can sign it and I'll send it on to HR.

Alex: Should I keep a copy?

Manager: If you like, I don't see the need. HR will send you a copy before next year's review if we're still here! Now let's get back to doing what we get paid to do.

What happens next?

Once the review meeting is complete, the real work begins. The meeting's true value will materialise post-meeting if you follow through with the agreed actions. During the meeting both parties made a series of commitments and recorded these agreements in their personal business plans (PBP). The question now becomes: "Do you keep your promises?"

Integrating the PBP into the day-to-day culture of managing your team requires a systematic approach to your follow-through. As outlined in **Chapter 1**, the reasons for the disconnect that exists between reviews and the day-to-day workings of the team include: 'it's an annual event', 'there is no follow-through' and 'the goals will change next month anyway'. These problems can be overcome when everyone takes responsibility for following up on their PBPs and delivering on their promises.

Keep in mind the principles of PEAK Leadership and how they can build on each other to promote a follow-through culture (see Figure 7.1).

Update everyone's SMARTER goals

In reality, business goals will change throughout the year. As with any change, you need to communicate these clearly. Inform your team when key priorities change so that they can alter their focus accordingly. Update critical goals as soon as possible so that your team are fully concentrating on delivering results that matter to your company.

Once you have communicated and agreed any change, update their personal business plans with the amended goals and new time frames. This quick exercise keeps the whole process relevant and up-to-date.

If some goals are no longer part of their review but they have put a lot of effort into them before the change, you should acknowledge this fact. Put a note on their PBP so that it will be recognised on their final report at the end of the year.

FIGURE 7.1 — PEAK LEADERSHIP

P

PERFORMANCE IS CHALLENGED

Introduce a systematic approach to implementing the action plans agreed with each member of your team. Make people accountable for broken promises.

E

ENVIRONMENT IS CREATED

Design a poster for the team that highlights the key business goals and their impact on the business. Ensure this poster can be updated easily as goals and priorities change. This will help in building a flexible culture within the team.

A

ALIGN THE GOALS

Show how each person will contribute to the team's success through their SMARTER goals. Give each goal a value and discuss the company's successes during the year by highlighting the team's (and individuals') contributions.

K

KEEP STAFF ENGAGED

After each monthly team meeting, update the poster by showing the progress being made against the target. Reward the team's progress.

Quarterly reviews

Quarterly reviews ensure that key priorities are followed-up and that the whole process is meaningful and productive. It brings both clarity and accountability to your performance management process by connecting these meetings to your day-to-day business discussions with your team.

These meetings should be scheduled at the beginning of the year (at the end of your first review meeting) and last approximately 20 to 30 minutes. The purpose here is to stand back from the day-to-day activities and think more strategically.

Figure 7.2 shows what should be included on the agenda for the quarterly review meeting.

FIGURE 7.2 — AGENDA FOR QUARTERLY REVIEW MEETING

UPDATE ON QUARTERLY RESULTS FOR COMPANY AND OVERALL CONTRIBUTION BY TEAM.

UPDATE ON PROGRESS OF SMARTER GOALS AGAINST TARGETS.

UPDATE ON THE ORGANISATION'S OVERALL BUSINESS PLAN AND ITS IMPACT ON THE TEAM.

UPDATE ON PERSONAL LEARNING AND DEVELOPMENT PLANS.

KEY PRIORITIES FOR NEXT QUARTER.

ANY OTHER TOPICS AGREED FOR DISCUSSION.

When the meetings are completed, update everyone's quarterly PBP document (see Figure 7.3) and forward them to HR. Keep a copy for your own records and give a copy to each person.

Follow through on training requests

Send a copy of everyone's personal learning and development (PLD) plans to HR or your training department so that they can coordinate the training requirements you and your team identified. Book all training events as soon as possible and schedule them on your team's yearly planner. This is an area that is often overlooked, so following through on your commitments to learning is important.

Avoid cancelling learning and development events, as it will create an impression that these sessions aren't considered important. Remember that nurturing your talent is part of the company's retention strategy.

Change in direction

At some stage during the year, people will move from or join your team. How you deal with this transition will have a big impact on performance levels and how quickly someone integrates into your team's culture.

When someone joins your team, begin on a positive note. As part of the induction process you should schedule a goal-setting meeting with them. This is a mini business review meeting, so it requires thorough preparation. During this meeting you will outline their SMARTER goals, your expectations for their overall performance and how their efforts impact the business. This ensures that a productive environment is created from day one.

When someone leaves your team, you should complete their review up to their date of transfer. Acknowledge their contribution and sign off on their performance. They have worked hard for you, so their efforts must be recognised. It increases the chances of high-performing people returning to work for you later in their careers. Complete this review even if they are leaving the company.

FIGURE 7.3 — TEMPLATE FOR THE QUARTERLY PERSONAL BUSINESS PLAN

<COMPANY LOGO>

QUARTERLY REVIEW UPDATE <PERIOD>

EMPLOYEE'S NAME	DEPARTMENT	MANAGER'S NAME

REVIEW OF SMARTER GOALS <PERIOD>

Summary of any changes to organisational business goals for <period>

COMPLETED SMARTER GOALS <PERIOD>

SUCCESS INDICATORS	SMARTER GOAL	BEST FEEDBACK	ASSESSMENT %
			EXCEEDED EXPECTATIONS ☐ MET EXPECTATIONS ☐ DID NOT MEET EXPECTATIONS ☐
			EXCEEDED EXPECTATIONS ☐ MET EXPECTATIONS ☐ DID NOT MEET EXPECTATIONS ☐
			EXCEEDED EXPECTATIONS ☐ MET EXPECTATIONS ☐ DID NOT MEET EXPECTATIONS ☐

FIGURE 7.3 CONT. — TEMPLATE FOR THE QUARTERLY PERSONAL BUSINESS PLAN

PERSONAL BUSINESS PLAN <YEAR>

Overall Feedback on Personal Business Plan <year>

EMPLOYEE COMMENTS:

Overall Feedback on Personal Business Plan <year>

MANAGER COMMENTS:

SUMMARY OF SCORING TO USE:

120%	EXCEPTIONAL PERFORMANCE – 120% OF TARGET
110%	EXCEEDS EXPECTATIONS – 110% OF TARGET
100%	MEETS EXPECTATIONS – 100% OF TARGET
90%	DOES NOT MEET EXPECTATIONS – 90% OF TARGET
80%	DOES NOT MEET MINIMUM STANDARDS – 80% OF TARGET

FIGURE 7.3 CONT. — TEMPLATE FOR THE QUARTERLY PERSONAL BUSINESS PLAN

NEW SMARTER GOALS FOR <PERIOD>

UPDATED KEY COMPANY GOALS <YEAR>

UPDATED KEY TEAM GOALS <PERIOD>

UPDATED SMARTER GOALS <PERIOD>

Success Indicators	SMARTER Goals	Key actions to take

UPDATED PERSONAL LEARNING AND DEVELOPMENT PLANS <PERIOD>

Learning & development needs identified	Alignment to business plan

<ADDITIONAL TOPICS AGREED ON AGENDA>

Further Comments

SIGNED (EMPLOYEE):	DATE:
SIGNED (MANAGER):	DATE:

4/15 report

Managing the performance of your team is an ongoing process, so review meetings should be integrated into your leadership style and the performance culture of your team. This isn't easy and it requires a disciplined approach. Completing a 4/15 report will support your efforts. A 4/15 report is simply answering four questions that will take no more than 15 minutes to complete. You can choose any questions that will improve the quality of your meetings.

FIGURE 7.4 — SAMPLE QUESTIONS FOR THE 4/15 REPORT

Do you update everyone's personal business plans when goals change?

Are all members of your team aware of and understand their success indicators?

Do you have a written performance improvement plan (PIP) in place for each underperformer?

Has everyone received some BEST feedback this week?

Do you conduct quarterly review meetings?

Do you have a structured programme of rewards and consequences for meeting or missing expectation levels?

How many people on your team right now aren't meeting your performance expectations?

How many of your team write their own SMARTER goals?

Have you set performance expectations (success indicators) for all of your team?

A review meeting is more than just discussing goals

When used correctly and proactively, the review meeting ultimately ensures that your company has the best possible chance of delivering a sustainable level of high performance today and into the future. In most companies it is the primary tool used to communicate key business targets and to give feedback on performance. Figure 7.5 lists the compelling benefits of regular review meetings for your company and team.

FIGURE 7.5 — THE BENEFITS OF REGULAR REVIEW MEETINGS

THE BENEFITS OF REGULAR REVIEW MEETINGS

Top managers understand that review meetings are about more than just discussing people's targets and key objectives. They ensure that all of their team:

- Have a clear understanding of their SMARTER goals and how their goals are aligned with the overall business strategy.
- Are given feedback on their performance and shown where they have added real value to the team and company.
- Are given the opportunity to demonstrate why they are the best at what they do and what they will achieve this year.
- Have the necessary skills and knowledge to exceed their goals and thereby deliver a high performance.
- Are supported by management and the company in their personal learning and development and their future employability.
- Are part of the process of defining their development strategy and key goals.
- Are thinking like entrepreneurs in the workplace and have a positive impact on the business strategy.
- Have a clear understanding of what is expected of them, both in terms of results and how those results should be achieved.

AT A GLANCE — CHAPTER SEVEN

During the meeting both parties made a series of commitments to each other and recorded these agreements in their Personal Business Plans. The question now becomes: "Do you keep your promises?"

Update critical goals as soon as possible so that your team are fully concentrating on delivering results that matter to your company.

Holding quarterly review meetings ensures that key priorities are followed up and that the whole process is meaningful and productive.

When the meetings are complete, update everyone's PBP and forward them to HR. Keep a copy for yourself and give one to the team member.

Send a copy of everyone's PLD plans to HR or your training department so that they can coordinate all the training requirements.

At some stage during the year people will move from or join your team, so update their PBP before they leave. Introduce new team members to their PBP as part of their induction process.

Completing a 4/15 report will support your efforts to turn the review into a tool for managing people.

FINAL WORDS

Imagine if you were the manager of your local sports team and only two players knew your tactics and plans for the match and only three players were interested in or passionate about winning the game. You also didn't bother doing any coaching or training during the season because you didn't have time. Imagine that less than half the team understood their roles or how their performance impacted the rest of the team, no one kept score during the game and you didn't give the players feedback until the end of the season.

What are the chances your team would win a game, much less a championship? Slim, I'd reckon – this is a recipe for confusion and underperformance. You simply would not manage a sports team this way if you wanted to win. Yet in business, many people end up managing their teams the same way, because they don't understand the importance of performance management and, in particular, how to maximise the benefits of the performance review meetings. Performance management is about far more than ticking boxes on a form.

As a manager, you are entrusted with getting the best from your team. This starts with understanding how to get the best out of the performance review meetings to give you and your team the winning edge. The key tools explored in this book to help you succeed were as follows:

- ✓ SMARTER goal setting
- ✓ Performance alignment
- ✓ BEST feedback
- ✓ Coaching alignment
- ✓ Career alignment

APPENDIX A COACHING LOG

A personal learning and development plan that is used to develop a career path is the foundation of retaining your top talent. A vital step in imbuing these plans into the culture of your team is identifying the key areas where your support will be required. Consider how best to utilise your limited coaching time for each member of your team. To avoid a fragmented approach, use the following worksheet to record how you use your time and who benefits from your expertise.

COACHING UPDATE

MANAGER	NAME OF EMPLOYEE	DEPARTMENT	JOB TITLE

PERSONAL LEARNING AND DEVELOPMENT PLAN <PERIOD>

(INSERT DETAILS FROM EMPLOYEE'S PERSONAL LEARNING AND DEVELOPMENT PLAN)

Learning and development needs identified	Alignment to business plan

COACHING OPPORTUNITIES

(INSERT COACHING OPPORTUNITIES IDENTIFIED TO MEET THE ABOVE NEEDS.)

Event	Where	When

Coaching Outcomes (Insert what was learned.)	Coaching Applied (Insert how the coaching was applied, providing examples.)
DATE:	DATE:

APPENDIX B MENTORING LOG

As you develop your leadership skills and become a great manager, there comes a time in your career when you should consider giving something back to your organisation. One idea to consider is mentoring the next generation of managers. This is a great way to utilise your experience as a leader.

Use the framework below to add some structure to these mentoring meetings and to ensure that there are tangible benefits. Overall, the person you are mentoring should become better equipped with the skills and experience necessary to meet the challenges of managing people and delivering business results.

MENTORING UPDATE

MANAGER	NAME OF EMPLOYEE	DEPARTMENT	JOB TITLE

MENTORING PERIOD	DEPARTMENT

Success Indicators for Career
(Insert a brief description of the employee's career ambitions and what success looks like in terms of their career progression.)

SMARTER Goals
(Insert clear outcomes for the mentoring period.)

OUTCOME FROM MEETING 1

(Insert what was discussed, homework given to employee, purpose of homework, etc.)

DATE:

OUTCOME FROM MEETING 2

(Insert what was discussed, homework given to employee, purpose of homework, etc.)

DATE:

OUTCOME FROM MEETING 3

(Insert what was discussed, homework given to employee, purpose of homework, etc.)

DATE:

OUTCOME FROM MEETING 4

(Insert what was discussed, homework given to employee, purpose of homework, etc.)

DATE:

OUTCOME FROM MEETING 5

(Insert what was discussed, homework given to employee, purpose of homework, etc.)

DATE:

SIGNED (MENTOR):	DATE:
SIGNED (EMPLOYEE):	DATE:

REFERENCES

Arkin, A., "From Soft to Strong", *People Management*, 6 September 2007, Vol. 13, No. 18.

Armstrong, M., *Armstrong's Handbook of Human Resource Management Practice*, 11th Edition (Kogan Page, 2009).

Chartered Institute of Personnel and Development, "Performance Management in Action" (2009).

Drucker, P., *Managing for Results* (HarperCollins, 2006).

Fayol, H., *Administration Industrielle et Generale (General and Industrial Management)* Trans. Constance Storrs (Martino Fine Books 2013).

Gawande, A., *The Checklist Manifesto: How to Get Things Right* (Profile Books, 2009).

Henshaw, J., Learn in Just 10 Minutes… How to Run Motivational Performance Appraisal Meetings, Kindle Edition (Amazon Digital Services, 2013).

Locke, E. and Latham, G., New Developments in Goal Setting and Task Performance (Routledge, 2013).

Lombardi, M., *The Engagement/Performance Equation* (Aberdeen Group, 2011).

Lombardi, V., *What it Takes to be Number One: Vince Lombardi on Leadership* (McGraw-Hill, 2000).

Mercer.ie, "Snapshot Survey 2011: Employee Rewards, Benefits and Engagement" (March 2011).

McLoughney, S., *Slave to the Clock, Master of Time* (Chartered Accountant Ireland, 2008).

Michelli, J., *The Starbucks Experience: 5 Principles for Turning Ordinary into Extraordinary* (McGraw-Hill, 2007).

Page, R., *Hope is Not a Strategy* (McGraw-Hill Professional, 2002).

Pietersen, W., "Translating your strategy into a compelling leadership message" (*The European Business Review* 2010).

Prone, T. and Lyons, K., *This Business of Writing* (Chartered Accountants Ireland, 2006).

Reid, M.A. and Barrington, H., *Training Interventions*, 6th Edition (Chartered Institute of Personnel and Development, 1999).

Rotella, B., *Golf is a game of confidence* (Pocket Book, 1996).